D1608455

Teddy Bear

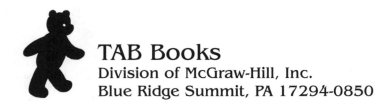

TAB Books
Division of McGraw-Hill, Inc.
Blue Ridge Summit, PA 17294-0850

Dedication

We would like to dedicate this book
to all those teddy bears out there!

Acknowledgments

We would like to thank:
Tracy A. Emmision for the Humbrol paints
Draper Tools for the scroll saw
Loctite for the Super Glue 3
Henry Taylor for the gouges and lathe tools

WE ALL LOVE BEARS! Pooh Bear, Paddington Bear, Goldilocks and the Three Bears, pictures of bears on cereal boxes, Yogi Bear, Rupert Bear, Sooty Bear, and Barney Bear—teddy bears in all their guises are beautiful!

Toys featuring bears have been around for a great many years: There are eighteenth-century German and Russian carved wooden bears, early nineteenth-century American tinplate money-box bears, and a great many other toys that draw their inspiration from all manner of black, white, and brown bears. However, the "Teddy" bear wasn't born until 1903 when an American cartoonist, Clifford Berryman, published a political cartoon in the *Washington Post* showing President Theodore "Teddy" Roosevelt refusing to shoot a bear cub. On seeing the cartoon, a certain Morris Michtom, founder of the American toy firm Ideal Toy Corporation, wrote to the President asking if he had any objection to him marketing one of his bear toys as Teddy's Bear. Roosevelt gave the go-ahead, and the rest, as they say, is history.

Okay folks! It's time to meet the most beautiful, the most brilliant, the brightest, the brainiest, the best-ever family of wooden teddy bear toys—the fabulous, the fantastic Bridgewater bears! These bears can balance, swing, trundle around in cars, fly around in planes, and perform teddy bear feats of daring action that will astound the eye and gladden the heart.

We would like to introduce you to a whole clan of truly original wooden teddy bear toys. There are fourteen projects in all. Each project opens with a tale for the tots and then the project goes straight into all the wonderful wooden toymaking procedures.

Now, we know that there are a lot of never-done-it-before beginners out there who have doubts—Are the toys too difficult? Are the techniques too complicated? But don't worry because within each of the projects, you'll find enough color photographs, project pictures, gridded and scaled working drawings, design templates, details, tools and material lists, and how-to drawings to guide you every step of the way. At the end of each project, you'll find a "special tips" section to sort out your queries and to help you over possible problems and pitfalls. And, just to put cream on the gingerbread, at the end of the book, there is an A–Z tools, tips, terms, and techniques section to ensure that nervous beginners are clued up.

We've included enough challenging, skill-stretching toymaking, woodworking techniques, ideas, designs, and details to keep even the most ardent, avid, and adventurous toymaker busy and satisfied. No matter what your particular woodworking interest—designing, drawing, using the scroll saw, drilling, cutting, carving and whittling, using the lathe, or whatever— each and every project has been very carefully considered so that the teddy bear toys can be shaped, modified, and adjusted to suit your own tool and skill level.

When you look through the projects, you will see that we have used a broad range of tools and techniques. Our thinking isn't that you should necessarily work each project in an entirely different way, but rather that you should study the project details, weigh up the possibilities in the light of your own tool kit and woodworking know-how, and then choose the approach that best suits you.

The tales for tots at the beginning of each project set the scene by giving the various teddy bears names and characters. The idea is that—if you can be persuaded to part with your ursine friend—when you hand the bear over, you can stimulate the children's imagination by also telling them as much as you can about the teddy, such as its characteristics, the name of the bear, its occupation, and so on. All the kids in your neighborhood are going to want one of your wooden teddy bear toys, and parting is such sweet sorrow. But just think how quickly you, the teddy, and the child will settle down and recover from the trauma when you introduce the bears to the kids by name!

If you like teddy bears, and if you are looking to make uniquely beautiful wooden toys, and if you want to learn as much as possible about a full range of wooden toymaking techniques, then *Teddy Bear Treasures* is for you.

Teddy bear gymnasts

ONCE UPON A TIME, there were ten little teddy bear gymnasts—five little boys and five little girls. Their names were Alan, Gillian, Glyn, Julian, Peter, Lorraine, John, Amy, Deborah, and Arlene. One day they decided to try and balance one on top of another to form a pyramid. Alan Bear, Glyn Bear, Julian Bear, John Bear, and Peter Bear held hands while Gillian Bear, Lorraine Bear, Amy Bear, Deborah Bear and Arlene Bear started to climb on their backs.

Suddenly, Gillian Bear started to wibble, and then Amy Bear started to wobble, and then, before you could say "wibble wobble" ten times over, the ten little teddy bears were all in a wibbly-wobbly heap on the floor . . . Crash!

> Ten little teddy bears
> A brave little band
> Ten little teddy bears
> Holding hand to hand
> Ten little teddy bears
> Climbing oh so high
> Ten little teddy bears
> Tumble from the sky!

This set of teddy bear gymnasts is a flatwood, locate-and-balance building toy made using a scroll saw and multicore plywood, using the techniques of fretting, laminating, and painting.

Materials

Best-quality multicore birch plywood
¼" thick 12"×24" for all the outside teddy bear cutouts
⅛" thick 12"×24" for the inside teddy bear cutouts
Sycamore/birch veneer
12"×12" for the paint and varnish compensating-thickness piece
Wood filler
Workout & tracing paper
Pencil & ruler
Package of short panel pins
Graded sandpapers
Loctite Super Glue

Acrylic paints (we use Humbrol matte acrylic colors)
Small can of clear, high-shine varnish

Small pin/peen hammer
Long-nosed pliers
Fine-toothed flat-bladed saw (such as a crosscut saw)
Electric scroll saw with a pack of fine blades (We used a Draper fretsaw)
Soft-haired paintbrushes, broad & fine

The teddy bear gymnasts are a cross between puzzle pieces, play bricks, and little hold-in-the-hand cuddle toys. They are just the right size for small, learning hands. With their bright imagery, the play possibilities are endless.

The little teddy bear shapes can be set flat down arranged in patterns, they can be stacked like bricks, they can be played with as individual pocket-type toys, and, best of all, they can be variously arranged, stacked and tessellated to make towers and pyramids. The intriguing three-thickness sandwich construction, with the central layer being set back slightly, allows the shapes to be locked and located edge-to-edge. All-in-all, the teddy bear gymnasts are challenging and good fun—the perfect toy for toddlers.

Have a good look at the working drawing shown on page 4 and note how each teddy bear is made up from five individual cutouts: two large "outside" bears cut from ¼-inch-thick ply, two "inside" bears cut from ⅛-inch-thick ply, and a single "center" bear cut from veneer. The function of the veneer is to compensate for the built-up thickness that will occur once the wood has been painted and varnished. This means that if the forms are to link edge-to-edge, the veneer makes the width of the inside layer slightly wider than the outside layer. Of course, you could reduce the outside ply thickness by sanding, but then again sanding is messy and time-consuming.

If you look at the design templates on page 5, you will see that we have achieved the slightly thicker inside layer by adding the single veneer to the two layers of ⅛-inch ply. We used the two

4 grid squares=1 inch

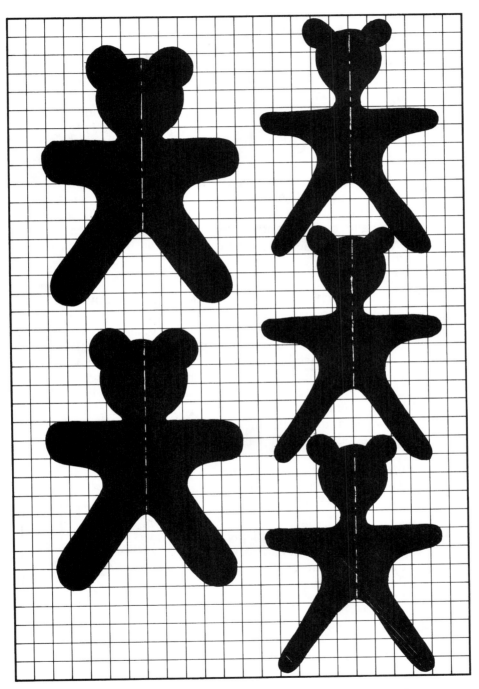

Teddy bear gymnasts   5

⅛-inch thicknesses rather than the single ¼-inch thickness because the veneer is so much easier to cut when it is sandwiched.

This is one of those beautifully flexible projects that allows plenty of room for design modifications. The bears can be bigger, smaller, thicker, or thinner, so it's best to look at your available materials and then to change and modify the specifications to suit your needs.

Skill level

If you like working on a small, tight, precise scale, and if you have the use of an electric scroll saw, then this is perhaps one of the most straightforward projects in the book. That said, if you have to use a handsaw and if you are not so keen on making repeats, then it could well be that this is not the project for you!

Setting out the wood

When you have had a good, long look at the various working drawings and details, to the extent that you have a clear understanding of just how the project needs to be worked and put together, draw the design up to full size and make clear tracings. You need two tracings, one of the outside bear, and one of the thinner inside bear. Note that the bear shapes are cut out in pairs, and make sure that the plywood is free from knots, stains, and delaminations. Next, take the ¼-inch-thick plywood, and use the ruler to set it out so that you have 20 little rectangles that measure 3"×4".

With the outside bear tracing, carefully pencil-press transfer the traced profile through to 10 of the rectangles. When you have achieved 10 crisply set-out images, set each of them on a plain rectangle so that the bear profile is uppermost, as shown.

If all is well, you should now have 10 paired rectangles. When you are happy with the arrangement, take the hammer and the pins and, making sure that the pins occur within the bear profile, carefully tack each pair of rectangles together with two pins.

Repeat this whole procedure with the ⅛-inch-thick plywood and the veneer—10 paired plywood boards and 10 veneers. This time, have a sheet of veneer filling in each of the plywood sandwiches, and trace the small teddy shape onto the top layer.

Having made sure that the scroll saw is in good working order and that the blade is nicely tensioned, take the pinned-up plywood sandwiches a piece at a time and carefully run them through the saw. It's all pretty straightforward, as long as you feed the wood into the blade at a steady, even pace, all the while making sure that the line of cut is a little to the waste side of the drawn line.

Using the scroll saw

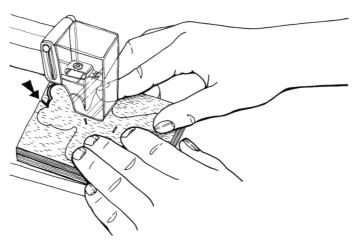

As you cut each pair of outside bears or threesome of inside bears, run pencil lines across the cut edges— one line on the first group, two lines on the second group, three lines on the third group, and so on— so that if there is a mix-up, you know precisely how the cutouts need to be regrouped and placed. It's best to cut out a group, mark the edges, and then put it carefully to one side.

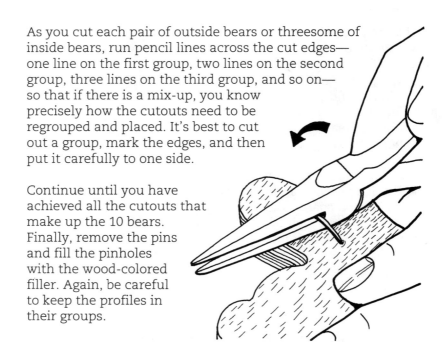

Continue until you have achieved all the cutouts that make up the 10 bears. Finally, remove the pins and fill the pinholes with the wood-colored filler. Again, be careful to keep the profiles in their groups.

Assembly

Give the pieces a swift rubdown with the fine-grade sandpaper to remove all the sharp edges and the excess filler. Then clear the worksurface of clutter, dust, and debris. This done, set the ply and veneer sandwiches on the bench and arrange them in groups for best fit.

Starting with the inner sandwich, one sandwich at a time, dribble a small amount of Super Glue around the edge of mating surfaces and stick the layers together. Press the pieces firmly together, but not so hard that you twist the shapes out of kilter.

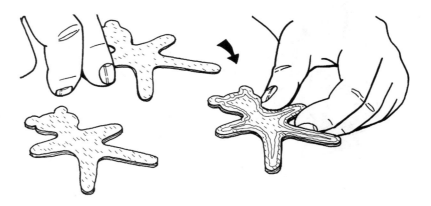

You can have the veneer sandwiched between the ply, or the two ply sheets together and the veneer to one side. It doesn't matter as long as the three layers are nicely aligned to make up a total thickness of a little over ¼ inch.

Next, continue the gluing procedure, only this time, of course, sandwich each inside lamination between two outside teddy cutouts to make the finished bear. If all is correct, the outside profiles should be nicely aligned and each bear should have a total thickness of just a fraction over ¾ inch. It's very important that the teddies stand up squarely, so spend time getting it right.

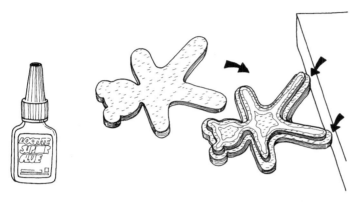

When the glue is dry, remove any dribbles with a knife, and sand all surfaces smooth. When you are happy with all ten bears, take a tracing from the painting grid, shown on the bottom right of the illustration on page 4. Carefully pencil-press transfer all the details of the face, shorts, and vest through to both sides of each of the bears.

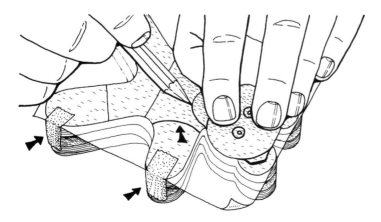

Painting Next, move to the area set aside for painting and paint in all the details that make up the design. Use the fine-point brush to paint the face details in fine black line, and paint the shorts and vest in bold blocks of color. If you look at the photograph of this project in the color section, you will see that we have limited ourselves to black, white, red, yellow, pink, green, and blue, swapping the colors around to make striking combinations. Leave the body of the bear unpainted.

Decorate both sides of all 10 bears, and allow the acrylic paints to dry completely. Next, being sure you sand between coats, give all the surfaces a couple of coats of clear varnish. It's best to first varnish the edges and then one side. Then, when that varnish is dry, turn the bear over and varnish the other side. Working in this way, you will always be able to set the half-varnished items down on the worksurface without worrying about the varnish sticking.

Finally, give the bears a swift rub-over with a small amount of furniture wax—just enough to reduce the friction of the fresh varnish—and the bears are ready for their act!

Special tips
- It is vital that you use best-quality multicore birch plywood. Be warned: If you use Malaysian "soft heart" types, the edges will be so soft and crumbly and almost impossible to sand smooth that the project will be a mess.
- If you use the finest piercing blades, the sawn edges will be so crisp and clean that you will be able to settle for a minimum of sanding.
- It's best to use brass pins so you don't have to worry about rust marks.
- We use Loctite Super Glue 3 because it is swift and instant—no mess, no ooze, and no fussing around with clamps. That said, you do have to make sure that the alignment is good the first time around because you don't get any second chances.

Three Bears puzzle

ONCE UPON A TIME, there were three bears who lived in a little cottage in the woods. One day they were out walking, when all of a sudden, the sun disappeared behind a big black cloud, the wind started to blow, and the rain started to splitter-splatter. Soon they were quite lost.

"Where are you?" cried Baby Bear.

"Hold my hand," said Mommy Bear.

"Oh dear, oh dear, we must not become separated!" growled Daddy Bear. Well, as you can see the three bears did become separated! Do you think you can put the three bears back together again?

> Daddy Bear big
> Mommy Bear round
> Three bears lost
> Three bears found!

This puzzle is a traditional flat-wood-framed jigsaw with Three Bears imagery. The project requires the use of a scroll saw and multicore plywood, and it centers on fretting and painting techniques.

Materials Best-quality multicore birch plywood (amount listed allows for small amount of all-around waste)
    1" thick 7"×10" for the figure layer
    ⅛" thick 7"×10" for the base layer
Workout & tracing paper
12 short panel pins/brads
Graded sandpapers
Glue (We used Loctite Rapid-dry glue)
Acrylic paints in red, light blue, dark blue, yellow, green, white and black (We used Humbrol matte acrylics)
Small can of clear, high-shine varnish

Tools Small pin hammer
Long-nosed pliers

Electric scroll/fretsaw with a pack of fine blades
Hand drill with a ¹⁄₁₆" diameter drill bit
Pencils, soft & hard
Ruler
Compass
Try square
Soft-haired paintbrushes, broad & fine

Looking & planning

The Three Bears puzzle is a really beautiful, educational toy. Look at the project picture on page 11 and see that it's more than just a puzzle. Once out of the frame, the individual pieces can be made to stand up and swapped around to make any number of funny character bears, as shown on page 14. For example, you might fit Daddy Bear's trousers, Mommy Bear's blouse, and Baby Bear's head together, or Baby Bear's legs, Daddy Bear's chest, and Mommy Bear's head together, and so on.

Have a close look at the working drawings to see how the head-to-body and the body-to-leg curves have been drawn with a compass and designed so that the puzzle components are interchangeable and come together for a good fit. All in all, this is the perfect toy for preschool kids. Give this puzzle to the average 4- to 6-year-old, and they will derive a lot of giggly pleasure as they build the funny figures. Another big plus is that the kids will also be able to test out their how-does-it-fit skills when they put the puzzle pieces back in the frame.

Study the working drawings on page 15 and the details, and consider how the puzzle is made up from two layers, the 1-inch-thick figure layer and the ⅛-inch-thick base board. Note the use of compass curves for the through-body lines and the little finger holes. See also how the finger holes make a very nice and convenient start point for the saw blade.

Although we used 1-inch ply for the figure layer, you can modify the project and laminate the thickness up from a number of thin layers. For example, if you can't use an electric saw, you might use a fretsaw or even a coping saw to work the figure layer from four ¼-inch thicknesses or two ½-inch thicknesses. This way of working is certainly going to result in a

Scale: 4 grid squares=1 inch

Scale: 4 grid squares=1 inch

lot of filling, sanding, and fussing about, but it's good manageable way of making the project with a modest tool kit.

Skill level

If you have the use of an electric scroll saw and if you enjoy working on swift, finished-in-a-day projects, then I would say that this is the project for you. That said, because the design is so bold in its shape, size, and number of the pieces, the cutouts need to be taken to a good, round-edged finish, and the painting needs to be carefully managed. It needs thinking about!

Setting out

When you have a clear understanding of just how the project needs to be worked and put together, draw the design up to full size, and make a clear tracing of the front and back sides of the bear.

This done, carefully pin together the two sheets of plywood with a couple of pins or brads. Using the pencil, ruler or try-square, and compass, very carefully set out the size of the frame at 6 inches wide, 9 inches long, with 1-inch radius corner-curves. Spend time making sure that all the lines and curves are crisply established.

When you are happy that all is correct, move to the scroll saw. Make sure the blade is nicely tensioned and the saw is generally in good working order. Then switch on the power and set to work cutting out the frame and clearing away the waste. It's all simple enough, as long as you feed the wood into the saw blade at a nice, easy pace, all the while adjusting the direction of approach and the rate of feed so that the saw is always presently with the line of next cut, and so that the line of cut is a little to the waste side of the drawn line shown on page 17.

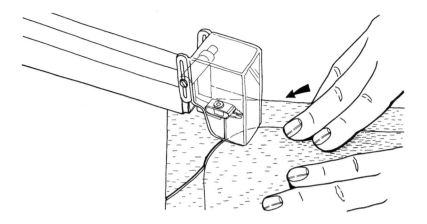

Finally, when you have fretted out the round-cornered frame shape, draw a couple of pencil registration lines on one side edge. Then carefully ease and remove the tacking pins with the long-nosed pliers.

Set the 1-inch-thick slab top-face-up on the workbench, and position the traced design of the front view of the three bears on the top face. Hold this in place with four tabs of masking tape, and use a hard pencil to press transfer the primary traced lines through to the wood. Again, it's worth spending the time to make sure that all the lines are crisply and clearly established. When you have removed the tracing, you might need to go over the lines with a soft pencil.

Drilling & fretting

Next, mark in the center points of each of the three finger holes, and run them through with the 1/16-inch-diameter drill bit.

Return to the scroll saw. Slacken off the blade tension, unhitch the blade, and pass it through one or other of the pilot holes.

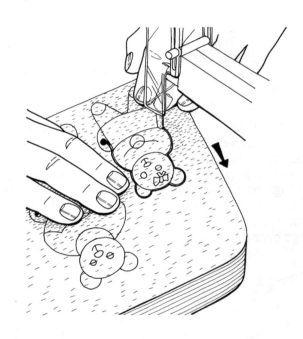

Then hitch up and re-tension, and fret out the bear shape as shown. Repeat this procedure for all three bears.

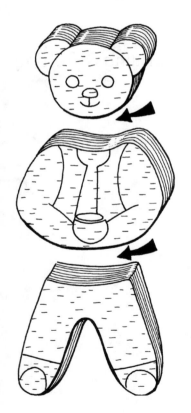

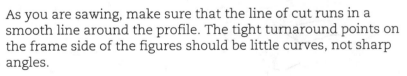

As you are sawing, make sure that the line of cut runs in a smooth line around the profile. The tight turnaround points on the frame side of the figures should be little curves, not sharp angles.

When you have cut the bears out of the frame, transfer the back design onto each bear. Then cut each bear into three parts as shown. If all is well, the three cutouts should be able to stand on their own feet, and the waist and neck curves should be such that the torsos and the heads can be swapped around.

Finally, take a sheet of fine-grade sandpaper and rub the whole workpiece—the frame and all the components that make up the three bears—down to a smooth, round-cornered finish.

NOTE: The finished pieces need to be a loose and easy fit to allow for paint and varnish buildup.

Clean up all the dust and debris, and then move to the clean, dust-free area that you have set aside for painting. Start by giving all the faces and sides of the work a thin sealing coat of clear varnish. When this coat is completely dry, go well away from the painting area and give the wood a swift rubdown to remove the *nibs*—meaning the grain hairs and whiskers—and glue and pin the baseboard onto the frame as shown.

Painting

Now, back in the painting area, study the painting grid shown on page 20. Using the soft-haired brushes and the matte acrylic paints, carefully block in the main areas of color: Daddy Bear's green trousers and red vest, Mommy Bear's blue dress, Baby Bear's yellow dress with the large white polka dots, and so on. Use the fine-point brush to dot and line in the small details. When you come to painting the frame, just settle for painting the top face and the outside edges blue.

When the acrylic paints are completely dry, give all surfaces—except the edges of the bear holes within the frame—another coat of varnish. Finally, give the inside edges of the holes a

Scale: 4 grid squares=1 inch

swift wax polish, just enough to reduce any friction. Now the bears are ready to puzzle over and play with!

- If you like the idea of the three bears but want to go for a more complicated puzzle, you could consider modifying the design so that the bears break down into a greater number of parts. Or you could cut up the puzzle parts so that there are link-up points, as in traditional jigsaw puzzles.
- When you are painting and varnishing, be careful not to lay on so much paint or varnish that the figures are too tight a fit in their holes. Watch out for paint/varnish buildup on the cut edges.
- Because the bear figures are more or less symmetrical ones, we realized they might get jammed if they were fitted backwards into the puzzle holes. To avoid this problem, we decided to give the bears a positive, easy-to-recognize back and front imagery—faces, arms, feet at the front, and so on.
- In many ways, the finger holes are more a convenient position for the pilot holes than they are functional, easy-to-hold holes for kiddies' fingers. You could improve the design slightly by having finger holes at several points around the figures.

Bengee Bendy Bear

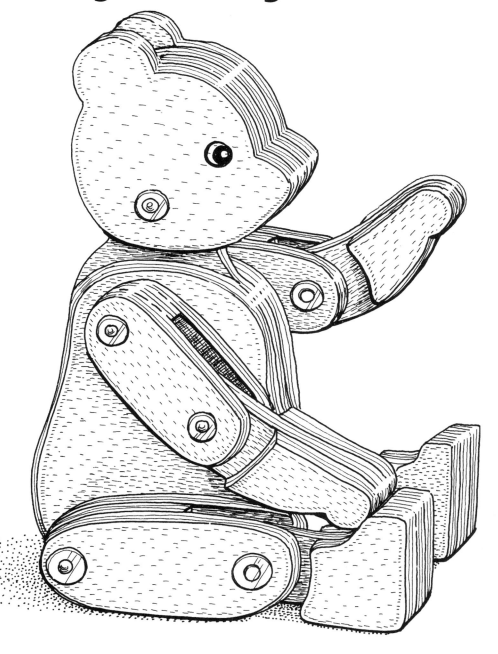

ONCE UPON A TIME, there was a little teddy called Bengee Bendy Bear. Bengee was an acrobatic tumbler. "I can touch my toes, I can roll up in a ball, I can do almost anything," boasted Bengee Bear as he huffed and puffed through his early morning workout.

"But can you stand on your head?" asked a mischievous friend.

"Well, I'll try," laughed Bengee. As he twirled and cartwheeled across the garden in readiness for his headstand, Bengee Bear sang a little song:

> Jumping and running are good fun
> Gymnastics is my game
> Tumbling turns are what I do
> Bengee is my name!
>
> The sky is blue
> The sun is red
> Do look at me
> I'm on my head!

Bengee is an articulated jointed flatwood toy. The pivots allow the limbs to be bent. For this project, you will need a scroll saw, a drill, and a rivet set. Bengee is made from multicore plywood, and the project involves fretting, riveting, and varnishing techniques.

Materials
Best-quality ¼"-thick birch multicore plywood, about 9"×12" (this allows for a good deal of cutting waste)
Five 1"-long ⅛"-diameter flat-head rivets for the neck, elbow, & knee joints
Ten washers to fit rivets
Two 3"-long ⅛"-diameter slot-headed machine bolts for the shoulder & hip joints
Twelve washers to fit machine bolts
Super Glue
Workout & tracing paper
Graded sandpaper
Matte acrylic paint
Clear, high-shine varnish

Small anvil/metal block/metalwork vise
Rivet set to fit/clench your chosen type of rivets
Small, ball-type hammer for spreading over the rivets
Pencil
Ruler
Electric scroll saw or fretsaw
Hand drill with ⅛"-diameter bit to fit
Fine-point craft knife
Soft-haired paintbrushes, broad & fine

Bengee Bendy Bear is an easy-to-make, good-fun toy. He is the type of toy that will give pleasure to children and adults alike. No noise, no cogs or springs, no batteries—just a simple little teddy bear figure that can be bent at the joints and set in all manner of funny positions as shown on page 26.

Have a good, long look at the working drawing on page 27. Note that the grid scale is 4 squares to 1 inch, or 1 grid square to ¼ inch. Bengee Bear stands about 7 inches high from head to toes. This toy is worked from ¼-inch-thick multilayer plywood, with the neck/head, elbows, and knees arranged and layered like bridle joints and pivoted on soft tap-end rivets, while the shoulders and hips are pivoted on long machine bolts. Consider how Bengee Bear, because of his side-to-side thickness of nearly 2½ inches, is able to stand on his own two feet, or his head, or his hands, or just about any part of his body.

When you have a good understanding of how the project needs to be worked, decide if you want to copy our design. Of course, if you like the overall idea of the project but want to make modifications, now is the time to change the design.

For example, you might want to change the scale and have a bigger or smaller bear, or you might want to give him clothes, or a fatter body, or whatever. Spend time finalizing the design, drawing up material lists, and generally considering alternatives. Once you have explored all the possibilities, draw your profiles out to size.

Scale: 4 grid squares=1 inch

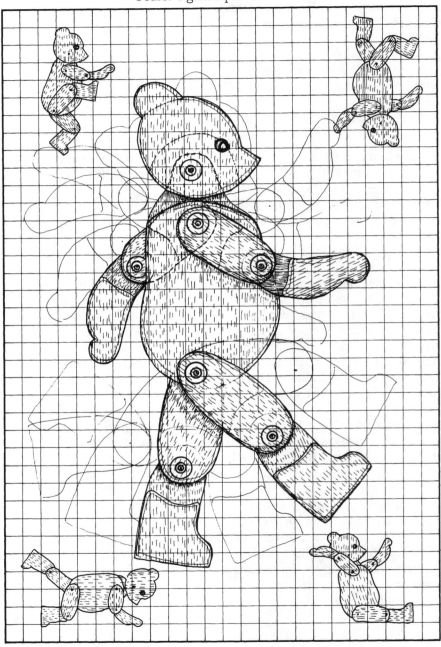

Scale: 4 grid squares=1 inch

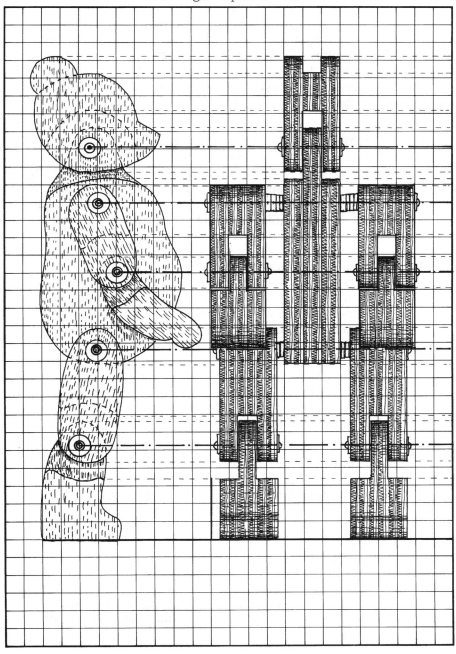

Skill level   The working stages are pretty direct and uncomplicated—just fretting, gluing, and drilling. However, I think it fair to say that the riveting does need to be very carefully managed and organized. It isn't that the riveting technique is especially difficult, but rather, it is the sort of task that is best worked with a friend. Ideally, you need one pair of hands to hold the workpiece, while the other pair of hands sorts out the rivets, the washers, and the hammer.

Setting out the designs   When you have a clear understanding of all the tool and material implications of the project, take a clear tracing of all the parts, using the illustration on page 29 as a guide. With the tracing paper held secure with tabs of masking tape, carefully pencil-press transfer the traced lines through to the working face of the ¼-inch-thick plywood. Make sure all the pivot holes are clearly marked.

This done, remove the tracing paper and rework the transferred lines so that there is no doubt about the correct profile. If necessary, shade in the areas that need to be cut away, and label the various forms "upper outside leg left," "inside head spacer," and so on. Punch center holes for the pivot joints.

With the profiles clearly established, check the scroll saw over to make sure that it is in good working order. Swiftly cut the wood down to easy-to-manage pieces, and then set to work cutting out the various shapes.

First cuts   As you begin cutting with the scroll saw, be careful not to force or twist the saw or you will break the blade. Work carefully around the forms, all the while making sure that the line of cut occurs a little to the waste side of the drawn line, as shown on page 30.

If you experience such nasties as wood judder, saw vibration, blade bending, or friction burning, then either change the blade or adjust the tension. More than anything, don't rush. Just feed the wood into the moving blade at a steady, even pace. Continue until you have cut out all the profiles that make the Bengee Bear.

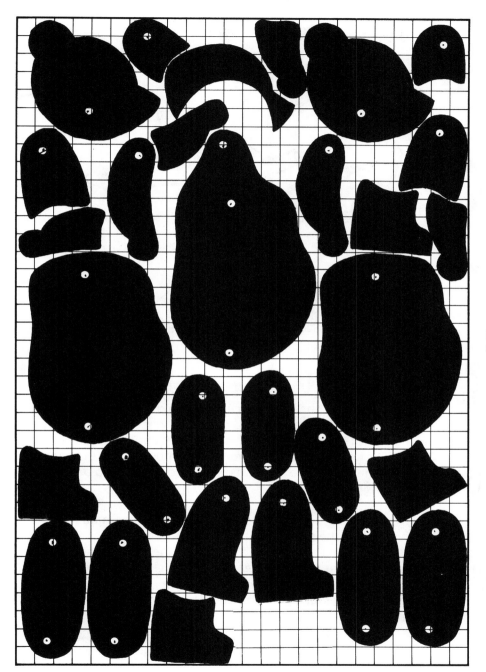

Scale: 4 grid
squares=1 inch

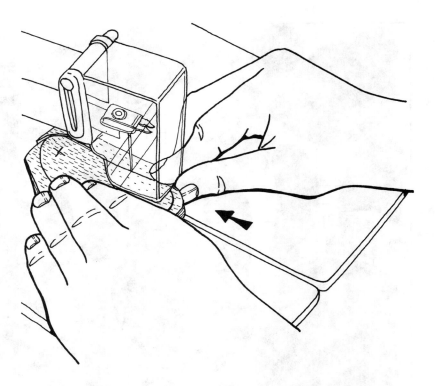

Gluing

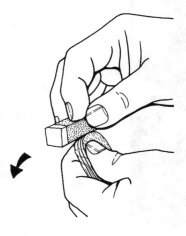

Set the cut pieces out on the bench. You should have 30 cutouts in all: the three pieces that make up the head, the two outside body pieces, the body-to-neck spacer, the six upper arm pieces, the six lower arm pieces, the six upper leg pieces, and the six lower leg pieces. Give all the cutouts a swift rubdown with the fine-grade sandpaper to remove all sharp burrs and cut edges.

Now smear glue on the mating faces of the two main body pieces and the middle-of-body neck spacer, and carefully set them together to make the three-thickness body as shown on page 31. Continue, one piece at a time, gluing all the other three-thickness components. When the glue is dry, have a trial assembly to make sure you know more or less what goes where and how.

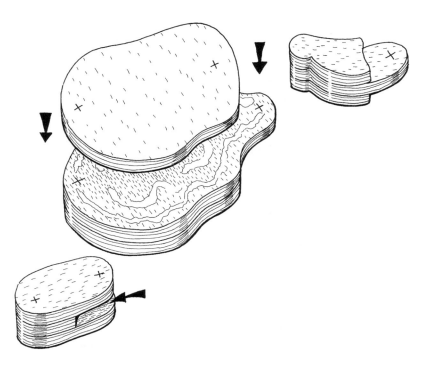

Having established how the bear fits together, take the sandpaper and, being careful not to lose the markings, swiftly rub down the inside-joint faces to loosen up the joints.

When you have achieved a good fit with all the joints, spend time establishing the exact position of the various pivotal rivet holes through the body and limbs.

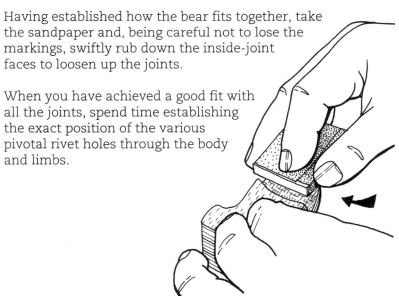

Drilling & sanding

Before you drill, slide a piece of ¼-inch-thick ply waste between the two joint layers of the head, the upper arms, and the upper legs so that you don't damage the unsupported face of the wood as the drill bit exits. This done, move to the bench drill and fit the rivet-sized drill bit. With the work carefully supported on a piece of scrap wood, run all the holes through, as shown.

Once you have worked the various pivot holes, move to the area that you have set aside for sanding. Rub all the components down to a smooth, round-edged finish. Clean out the drilled holes as shown, rub off all the cut edges, and generally work away at the wood until all edges and corners are smooth, nicely profiled, rounded, and completely toddler-sucking safe.

Painting & varnishing

When all the cutouts are absolutely smooth to the touch, clear away all the clutter and debris. Make sure that the work is free from dust, and retreat to the area that you have set aside for painting.

A word before you start: It's always a good idea to make checks to ensure that the painting environment is as near perfect as possible. The condition of the paint and varnish, the type of brushes that you are using, the amount of water in the air, the temperature, an impatient or nosy child—these are all factors that can affect the quality of the finish. The best advice is to take it slowly, a step at a time. Never skimp on the sanding, never mix different paint or varnish types, and always let the paint dry out thoroughly between coats. It's best to go for several thin coats rather than a single heavy daubing.

With all these cautions in mind, spend time arranging the component parts on a drying frame or line, as shown. Now, not forgetting to let the paint and varnish dry out between coats, lay on a thin coat of varnish. Give the surfaces a swift rubdown to remove hairs and nibs of grain.

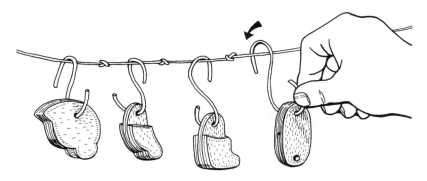

Next, use the fine-point brush and the black acrylic to paint in the eyes. Finally, lay on another couple of coats of varnish and let the pieces dry.

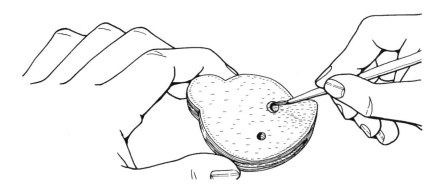

Riveting

Set out the painted components and be ready with the rivets, the washers, the metal block, the rivet set, and the hammer. Starting with the neck-to-head joint, slide a washer on the rivet, slide the rivet through the joint, and pop on another washer. The cross-section layers on the rivet should run:

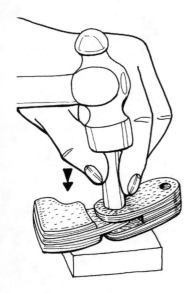

washer, the three layers of ply that make up the joint, and another washer.

When you are happy that all is correct, take the round-faced hammer and tap over the tail of the rivet with a dozen or so well-placed, glancing blows. Aim to spread the rivet carefully so that its tail is nicely rounded against the washer, as shown. This done, use the rivet set to shape and clench the mushroomed rivet.

When you have worked all eight rivets and have made sure that the joints are firm but flexible, fit the hip and shoulder joints with the nuts, the machine bolts, and the washers. Tap over the end of the thread so that the nuts stay put. Finally, lay on a last coat of varnish to make good any scuffs and scratches, and Bengee Bear is ready for his first workout!

Special tips

- If you want to make a larger or smaller bear, consider using a mixture of plywood thicknesses. So for example, you might have the body made from a single 1-inch thickness and each limb from three ⅛-inch thicknesses. Or then again, you could have the head, hands, and feet much thicker than the body.
- If you don't like the idea of using tap-end rivets, you might use pop rivets, glued dowels, or even nuts and bolts for all the joints.
- The joints need to be flexible, but not too tight or too loose. Consider using spring washers between the layers.
- When you are tapping over the tails of the rivets, you need to support the rivet heads on a metal sheet or block, and/or use a special rivet set. Ask your supplier.
- If you decide to use a slow-drying glue, then you will have to clamp up while the glue is curing.

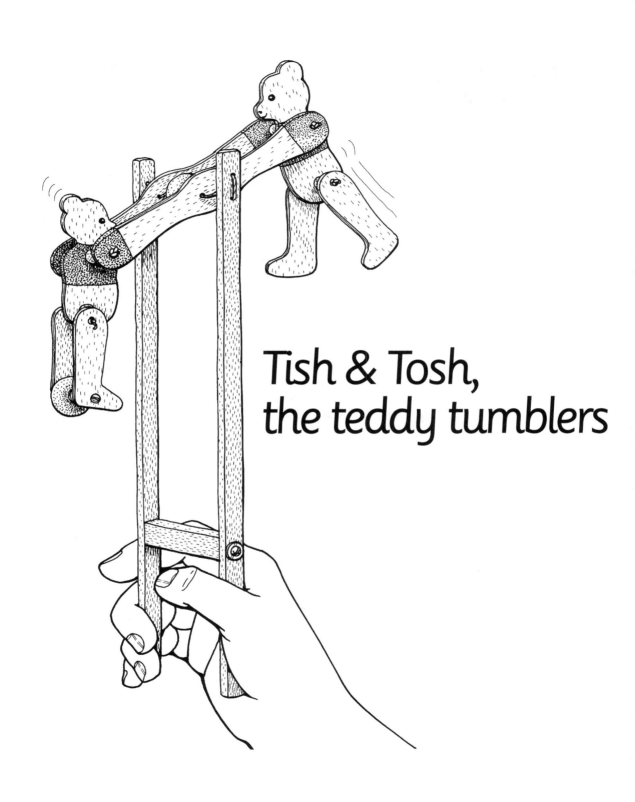

Tish & Tosh,
the teddy tumblers

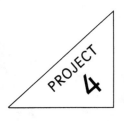

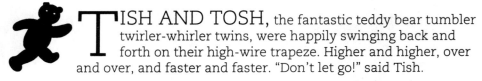

TISH AND TOSH, the fantastic teddy bear tumbler twirler-whirler twins, were happily swinging back and forth on their high-wire trapeze. Higher and higher, over and over, and faster and faster. "Don't let go!" said Tish.

"You must be joking!" said Tosh. Over and over they twirled and whirled, faster and faster, round and round, like rockets, like stars, like birds . . .!

> Twirling and whirling
> round they both go
> Tish and Tosh
> Are high and . . . then low!

> Over and over . . .
> Like birds in the blue
> Tish and Tosh
> Are flying . . . for you!

This toy consists of two twist-string pivotal figures. When the sticks are repeatedly squeezed, the two teddies flip backward and forward, over and over. For this project, you will need a fretsaw and a drill. The toy is made from multicore plywood and beads, using fretting, drilling, and painting techniques.

Twirler-whirler-type toys, sometimes called Merry Jacks, have been popular the world over for many years. We've seen country-rustic wind-driven whirlers that were made in 19th century America, pretty acrobats that were made in 18th century Austria, and little ivory figures that were made a hundred or so years ago in Japan. We could continue describing whirlers that were made in such faraway places as the Black Forest, Italy, Poland, Sweden, France, Russia, and just about every country that you care to mention.

Toys of this character take a bit of beating; they can be made from basic materials (thin wood and string), and their movement is both naive and ingenious. In use, when the sticks are squeezed together at the bottom, the bears set to twirling. An easy-to-make, popular toy that can be made swiftly at a low cost, this project has just got to be a good idea!

Best-quality birch multicore plywood, ⅛" thick, at about 6"×6" for the eight cutouts that make up the two figures
20" length of ⅜"×¼" section wood strip for the two squeeze-sticks (Use a smooth, knot-free wood, such as beech or jelutong.)
2" length of ½×⅜" section wood for the crossbar (You may use a small offcut.)
Four slender ¾"-long roundhead brass screws
Eight brass washers to fit screws
Two ¾"-diameter wooden beads
Eight ¼" plastic beads
Strong, fine nylon twine, about 36" allows for cutting and knotting waste
Graded sandpapers
Acrylic paint, red & blue
Clear, high-shine varnish
Super Glue
Workout & tracing paper

Fretsaw with spare blades
Birdsmouth cutting table (to be used with the fretsaw)
Small hand drill with a 1/16"-diameter bit
Small G-clamp
Soft-haired paintbrushes, broad & fine
Pencil
Ruler

Have a look at the working drawing on page 38. The grid scale is 4 squares to 1 inch, and the toy stands about 2½ inches wide and 12 inches high. Note such details as the use of ⅛-inch-thick multicore plywood for the teddy bear cutout, the simple easy-to-make string pivots, the loose screw-fixed crossbar, and the clever twist-string mechanism.

The heavy bear (the one with the ball bead between his feet) always pulls the seesaw arms down so that the twist-string mechanism is always wound up and ready to go. Consider also the way the loose-fixed bridge piece (the 2-inch length between the two sticks) acts as a fulcrum or lever point. The working action is beautifully simple: As the two sticks are squeezed together at the bottom, they open apart at the top, with the effect that the string unwinds and the teddies flip over as shown on page 39.

Tish & Tosh, the teddy tumblers   37

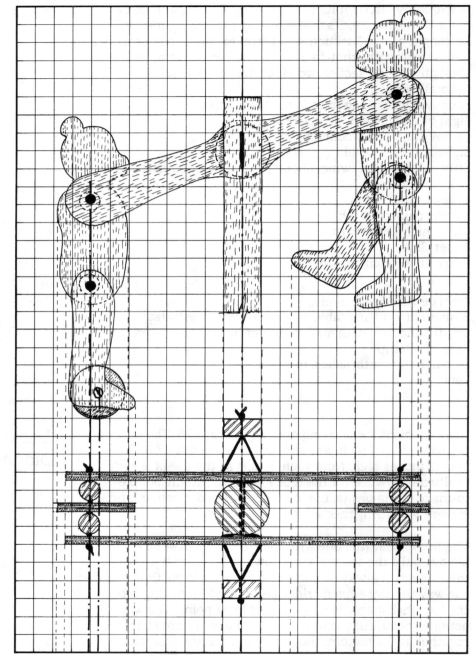

Scale: 4 grid
squares=1 inch

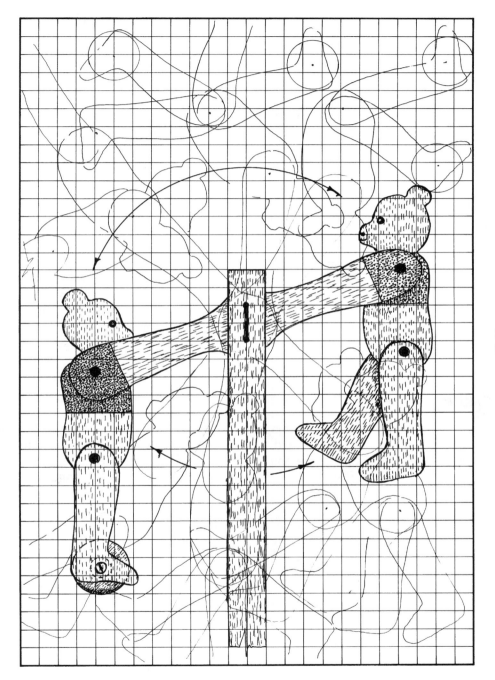

Scale: 4 grid
squares=1 inch

Tish & Tosh, the teddy tumblers   39

Skill level

This is the perfect project for the minimalist never-done-it-before woodworker in that it can be made with the simplest tools and materials. A fretsaw, a hand drill, a screwdriver, a paintbrush, and a few odds and ends of plywood and string, and you are well on your way.

That said, it is also one of those tricky finger-twisting little projects that requires a deal of small, tight fiddling around with lengths of string, sizes of knots, and weight before it all works out.

Setting out the design

Having studied the project picture on page 38 and the working drawings on pages 39, draw the design up to full size, using the pattern on page 41, and make a crisp tracing.

Next, pencil-press transfer the traced lines through to the working face of the ⅛-inch-thick plywood. You need two teddy bodies, four legs, and two seesaw arm shapes. Spend time getting it right the first time around, and make sure that all the pivot points are carefully and clearly established. Set out the two 10-inch-long squeeze-sticks and the 2-inch-long bridge between-stick piece.

Cutting & drilling

When you are happy with the way the profiles have been set out, clamp the birdsmouth cutting table to the edge of the bench, as shown on page 42 and set to with the fretsaw. It's all pretty straightforward, as long as the blade is well tensioned in the frame, and the point of cut is as close as possible to the vertex of the V of the birdsmouth table, as shown on page 42.

As you are working, run the line of cut a little to the waste side of the drawn line, and try all the while to keep the workpiece moving so that the blade is always presented with the line of next cut. Don't hurry or try to force the pace; just work steadily, turning the wood and maneuvering the saw, so that the cut runs at 90° to the working face of the wood. While the saw is at hand, cut the two squeeze-sticks and the little bridge piece to size.

Fix the position of the various holes. From stick to stick, you need to have a screw-fix hole for the bridge piece at a point

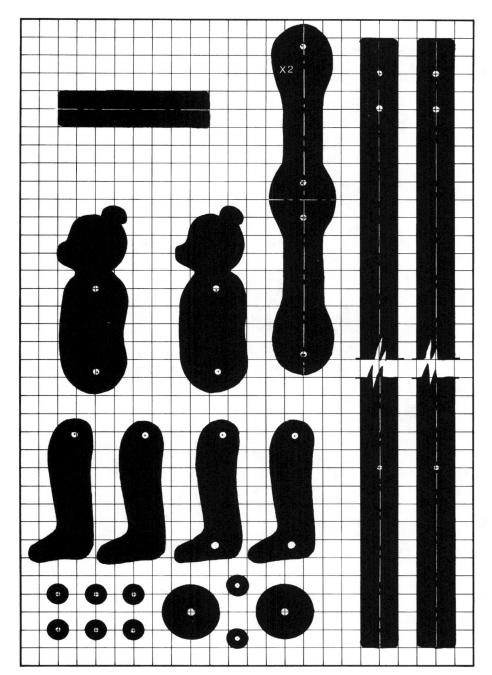

X2

Scale: 4 grid
squares=1 inch

Tish & Tosh, the teddy tumblers   41

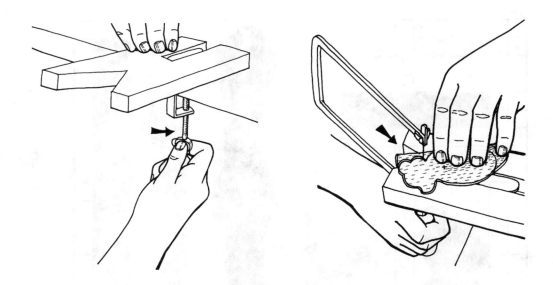

2½ inches up from the bottom, and two string holes ½ inch and 1 inch down from the top.

Having cut out all the component parts and established the position of all the holes, take the hand drill and the ¹⁄₁₆-inch-diameter bit and run all the holes through. Make sure that you support the workpiece on a piece of scrap wood so that as the drill exits, it leaves a clean-cut hole.

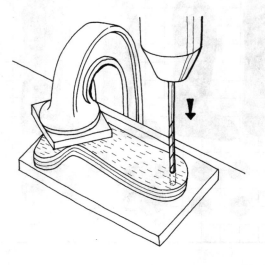

Finally, when you are happy that all is correct, take the fine-grade sandpaper and rub all 11 components down to a smooth, slightly round-edged finish.

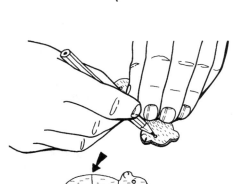

Clear away all the dust and debris, and move to the area set aside for painting. Start by drawing the small amount of imagery onto the cutouts: the T-shirts on the teddies, the T-shirt arms on the ends of the two seesaw arms, and the eye, nose, and mouth details on the faces.

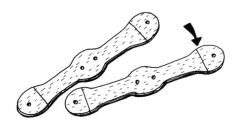

Next, use the fine-point brush to block in the flat areas of color—red for one bear and blue for the other. Pick out the face details with the black paint and the fine-point brush. When the

Painting & varnishing

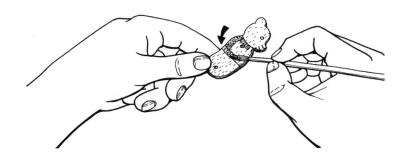

Tish & Tosh, the teddy tumblers 43

paint is completely dry and you are happy with the imagery, give the work a light sanding between coats. Then give all the components a couple of coats of clear varnish and put them aside to dry.

Making the frame

Take the two 10-inch lengths of ½-x-¼-inch section wood and the 2-inch-long bridge piece—all finished, drilled, and varnished—and check the position of the various holes that make up the design. When you have established that all is correct, fit the H frame together with the ¾-inch screws and the washers. Don't worry about the finished frame being a loose easy fit. This is how it needs to be.

Assembly

Having studied the working drawing on page 38 again, take the components one bear at a time, and carefully thread and knot the hip and shoulder pivot joints. The cord must be loose enough to allow for easy movement of the joint, so it's best to use a long length and then cut it back as necessary.

The sequence on the cord and through the joints is: limb, small bead, body profile, small bead, and limb. When you have checked that both bears correctly look to the center, knot the ends of the pivot cords and fix the knots with a small dab of Super Glue. It's a good idea to use a needle to pass the thread through the holes and to ease and adjust the knots.

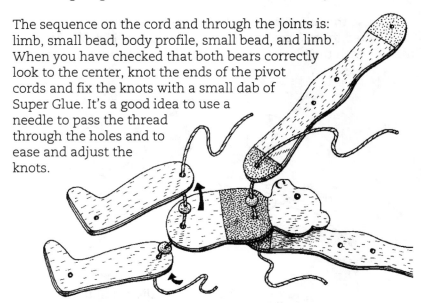

Take the bear with the
through-foot holes and
the ¾-inch-diameter
weight bead. Plug the bead
hole first with a match stick,
and then screw the feet to the
bead, with three washers at each
side of the bead, between the bead and
the foot, as shown. Note that the number of
washer-weights might need to be adjusted
at a later stage.

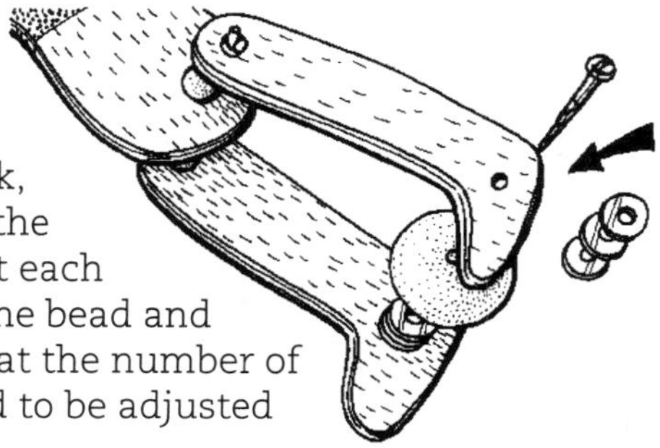

Now for the tricky bit. Set the H frame flat-down on the
worksurface, and arrange the bears on their backs so that the
unweighted, loose-footed bear has his feet down between the
long prongs of the H, and so all the hand holes are aligned. This
done, set the other ¾-inch-bead between the arms, and run a
length of cord from side-to-side through the frame, the arms,
and the bead.

Starting at the top hole on the frame, the cord should run
through:

1. the top hole
2. through the weighted bear's arm
3. through the bead
4. through the weighted bear's other arm
5. out through the top hole on the other side of the H frame
6. back through the second hole of the frame
7. through the other bear's arm
8. through the bead
9. through the other bear's other arm
10. out through the frame

When you have completed the loop, loosely knot it off.

If all is well, when you hold the H frame upright, the weighted
bear should always hang downwards so that there is a twist on
both sides of the cord loop. Starting with the bears looking at

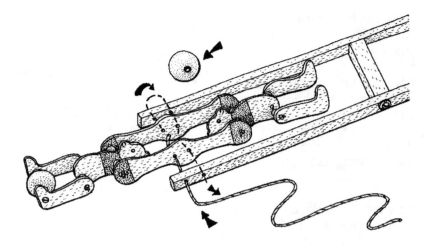

each other, when you squeeze gently on the bottom of the H frame, the top of the prongs should open out, causing the loop to untwist and the bears to flip over. Of course, as the bears flip over, the cord retwists and the bears will finish up back-to-back and looking away from each other.

You will almost certainly need to adjust either the length and slackness of the knotted loop and/or the number of washers on the weighted bear before you get the working action just right.

Finally, when you are happy that all is correct, fix the knots with a dribble of Super Glue, trim the cords to length, and Tish and Tosh are all wound up and ready to start the twirling and whirling action!

Special tips
- The measurement of the bear, from the tip of the toes through to the center loop point of the arms outstretched, must on no account be greater than the distance from the crossbar through to the top of the H frame.
- Don't be tempted to tidy up and glue-fix the loose-fitting H frame; it needs to be loose.
- Be warned: We fiddled around for some time before the working action was just right. Be ready with plenty of cord and a pair of helping hands to hold the components and to mop your brow!

Jolly
Jumping-
Jack Bear

JOLLY JUMPING-JACK BEAR

J OLLY JUMPING-JACK BEAR was just about as happy as happy could be. In fact, he felt so happy that he just wanted to buck, bounce, and bob up and down. The sun was shining, he had finished his work for the day, he had just eaten a huge cheese-and-chutney sandwich (the best food for jumping) and he was off to play in the yard.

Up and down, up and down . . . Jolly Jumping-Jack Bear was so excited that he just couldn't sit still. And as he bucked, bounced, and bobbed up and down, Jack sang a little song.

> Cheese and chutney
> Chutney and cheese
> I'll jump as much
> As I jolly well please
> I'll jump and jump
> When will I stop?
> I'll jump and jump
> Until I jolly well POP!

Jack is a traditional jumping-jack toy. When the string is pulled, the arms and legs flip up. This project involves the use of a lathe, a coping saw, a knife, and a drill. It's best made of American southern yellow pine, and making the toy requires turning, fretting, whittling, and painting techniques.

Materials

24" length of strong-grained easy-to-turn wood at 2"×2" square (We used American southern yellow pine.)
Strong fine twine, about 50" to 60"
Two ½"-diameter wooden beads
Four 1¼"-long panel pins
Super Glue (We used Loctite Super Glue 3.)
Workout & tracing paper
Wood filler
Matte black acrylic paint
Clear, high-shine varnish

Tools

Woodturning lathe with a four-jaw chuck to fit
A good selection of turning tools
Compass

Dividers
Calipers
Tenon saw
Coping saw
Small, sharp knife (for whittling)
Chisel, ¼"-wide
Drill with ⅛" & ⅜" bits
Small pin hammer
Soft-haired paintbrushes, broad & fine
Pencil
Ruler

Skill level

If you have the use of a medium-powered lathe (preferably one with a four-jaw chuck), if you enjoy working between centers, and if you are something more than a raw beginner, then this is the project for you. That said, I think it also fair to say that the putting-together stages do need to be worked with a deal of care and attention. It's most important that all the holes in the limbs and through the body be precisely placed.

Looking & planning

Jumping-Jack Bear is one of those archetypal, traditional toys that seems to delight children and adults alike. That is not to say that all jumping-jacks are bears or even round in section, but rather that such toys are characterized by having a one-piece head/body, arms that are pivoted at the shoulders, and legs that are pivoted at the hips. The toy can be held or hung, and at the pull of a string, the arms and legs flip up so that the figure looks to be jumping. It's a perfect toy to hang over a toddler's bed as a small play-and-cuddle toy.

Look at the project picture on page 50 and the working drawing to see how our Jumping-Jack Bear is special on many counts. He is beautifully rounded rather than the more usual, flat form. His arms and legs have been designed and stylized so that they are weighted at the extremities to give positive movement. The choice of wood, too, has been carefully considered so that the run of the grain adds to the overall texture and character of the form.

Note how the bear is made up from eight individual spindle turnings: the pear-shaped head, two discs for the ears, the

Jolly Jumping-Jack Bear 49

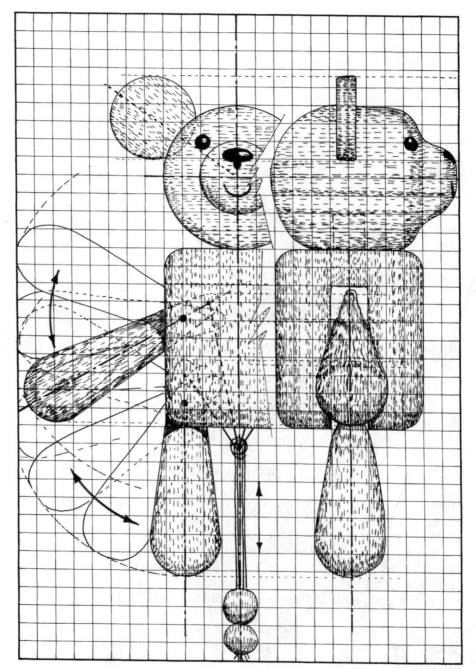

Scale: 4 grid
squares=1 inch

cylindrical body, and four identical baseball-bat-shaped limbs. Look at the details, and see the way the ear discs have been mortised into the head, the body slotted for the limbs, and the thin ends of the limbs whittled with the knife to give the round-section turnings two flat faces that fit into the body slot.

Consider how we have held and gripped the wood in a four-jaw chuck and turned the eight elements, like a string of beads, all from the same 24-inch length of wood. Of course, there's no denying that this way of working is slightly wasteful in its use of wood, but it is very economical in terms of time and effort. You need only to prepare and center once.

However, if you like the project, but don't have a four-jaw chuck or would prefer to use small scraps rather than one long piece, no problem. All you do is to work each component as a between-center turning or a small string of turnings, and modify the order of work to fit.

When you have studied the drawings and the working details to the extent that you have a clear understanding of how the bear needs to be turned, worked, and put together, check the 24-inch length of 2-x-2-inch-square section wood for possible flaws. If the wood is smooth, of a good color, and free from splits and knots, then no problem. If, on the other hand, there are end splits, stains, or awkwardly placed knots, or if the wood is in any way warped, twisted, or sappy, you should look around for another piece.

Preparing the wood

When you are happy that all is correct, establish the end-center points by drawing crossed diagonals, and then set the ends out with 2-inch-diameter circles. Draw tangents at the circle-diagonal crossover points, and establish the areas of corner waste by drawing lines from the resultant octagons and along the length of the wood. This done, take a plane or rasp and swiftly clear away the bulk of the waste.

Secure the wood in the jaws of the chuck and wind up the tail center. Set the tool rest slightly below lathe-axis height. Check with the pre-switch-on safety list (see glossary), and use the round-nosed gouge to swiftly turn the wood down to a round

Mounting & turning

section. Don't try too hard to achieve a perfect surface. Settle for a smooth cylinder that is more or less 2 inches in diameter.

Using a pencil, ruler, and dividers, set off the various lengths that make the bear. Follow the illustration, and from left to right, allow:

- 2 inches for chuck waste
- 2½ inches for the body
- 1 inch for waste and body/neck spigot
- 2½ inches for the head
- 1 inch for waste
- 3 inches for a limb
- ¼ inch for waste
- 3 inches for a limb
- ¼ inch for waste
- 3 inches for a limb
- ¼ inch for waste
- 3 inches for a limb
- ¼ inch for waste
- ¼ inch for one ear
- ¼ inch for waste
- ¼ inch for the other ear
- the final the remainder for the tailstock waste

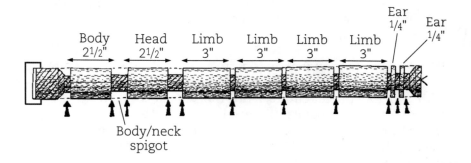

If all is well, you should have eight primary step-offs areas with small amounts of waste in between.

Check that all the step-offs are correct and then, with a slender parting tool, establish the length of the components by sinking cuts that are about ½ inch deep. This will leave you with a central core at about 1 inch diameter.

Next take the skew chisel and, starting with the bear's body, carefully turn off all the waste. Don't be in too much of a hurry to cut down to the envisaged form. It's much better to take it little by little and to gradually ease out the waste. As you are turning, always angle the tool so it cuts with the grain, from peak to hollow—or, you might say in this instance, from the body of the bear on down into the initial parting-tool cut.

When you have turned off the cylindrical round-ended shape of the body, then continue in like manner, turning the bear's head, limbs, and ears as shown.

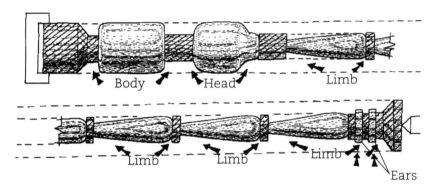

When you have achieved all the primary curves and forms (the curves on the body, the shape of the back of the head, the bear's nose, the bat shape of the limbs, and so on), turn the lathe down to a slower speed, and then use the calipers and the skew chisel to take the turnings to a good finish. Starting with one of the two ear discs, work from right to left, following this procedure:

1. Turn the ear disc down as close as you can.
2. Remove as much as possible of the waste.
3. Wind the tailstock back out of the way.
4. Position the rest over the bed of the lathe so that you can work the wood end on.

5. Carefully turn the face of the first ear down to a smooth finish.
6. Reposition the rest as before, and then part the ear off from the workpiece with the point of the skew chisel as shown.

When you have parted off the first ear, wind the tailstock back so that the workpiece is once again supported at both ends, and then work the other ear in like manner. Continue with the limbs, the head, and the body.

You must be very careful not to knock the wood off-center, and you might need to give the surfaces a swift rubdown with fine-grade sandpaper before the final parting off. The nearer you get to the headstock end of the lathe, though, the easier the whole operation becomes.

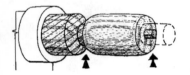

When you come to the head-end of the body, leave a ⅜-inch-diameter ½-inch-long spigot or stub for fixing the head to the body.

Cutting the body slot

Once you have worked, finished, and removed the turned components one by one from the lathe, take a scrap of sandpaper and rub the part-off points down to a good finish. Swiftly rub the base of the body turning down to a level finish, and mark in the top front centerpoint and the position of the arm and leg slot. The slot should start about ½ inch down from the top of body, and it should be ½ inch wide.

When you have marked in the position of the slot, set the body bottom-side-up in the jaws of a muffled vise, and use the tenon and coping saw to cut the waste. First use the tenon saw to run two parallel cuts straight down into the wood as shown. Then link the cuts up with the coping saw so that the slice of waste falls away.

Fitting the ears

This stage is difficult, so be warned and take it very slowly, one step at a time. On the head turning, first mark the position of the neck dowel-mortise hole, the eyes, the nose, and, of course, the two ears. Make sure that the strong lines of the grain run parallel and level with what will be the base or horizon line.

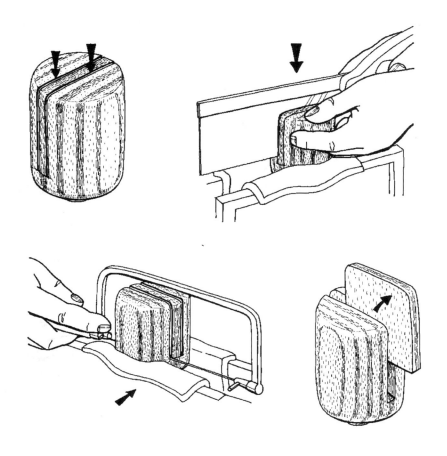

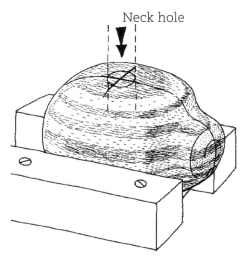

Neck hole

Then use the ⅜-inch drill bit to bore out the neck hole as shown.

Note that the ear discs are ¼ inch thick and about 1 inch in diameter. Use a pencil, ruler, and masking tape to establish the position of the ears on the head, as shown. The precise position of the ears isn't too important, as long as they are more or less on the same around-the-head line, and as long as they are placed symmetrically to the head centerline.

Ear placement

Use the saw and the chisel to scoop out the two little part-disc holes. (It's best to mark the two ears "left" and "right" and then cut each hole to fit.) Having defined the width of the slots with the saw, use a knife to deepen the slots, as shown. To remove the waste, support the head in one hand and the chisel in the other, and make a series of little scooping cuts.

Cut the slots and trim the ear discs to a good fit. Carefully note how you want the grain of the ears to run in relationship to the grain of the head. Then smear glue on mating surfaces, and set the ears in their slots. Drill a hole at top-of-head center, and glue the loop of hanging string in place. Dribble a small amount of glue on the neck spigot, and set the head in place on the body.

Shaping the limbs

All four limbs are identical in length (3 inches) and form. Using a pencil, mark in the length of the flattened inside-slot area. Set out the tapered end of the bat shape so that the flattened area is 1 inch long and about ¼ inch thick.

This puzzle is a traditional flatwood-framed jigsaw with Three Bears imagery. The project requires the use of a scroll saw and multicore plywood, and it centers on fretting and painting techniques.

Jolly Jack is a traditional jumping-jack toy. When the string is pulled, the arms and legs flip up.

This set of teddy bear gymnasts is a flatwood, locate-and-balance building toy made using a scroll saw and multicore plywood, using the techniques of fretting, laminating, and painting.

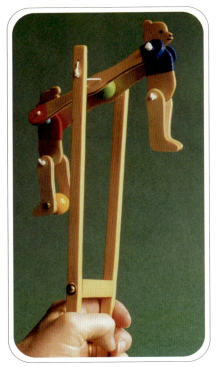

This clock with Betty Bear and balloon imagery is a project that emphasizes fretting and piercing techniques. It would be a delightful addition to a nursery or child's room.

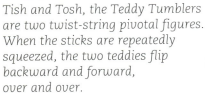

Tish and Tosh, the Teddy Tumblers are two twist-string pivotal figures. When the sticks are repeatedly squeezed, the two teddies flip backward and forward, over and over.

Larry the Lumberjack Bear is a traditional friction-climb toy. As the strings are pulled, the figure slowly climbs up the strings.

Bengee the Bendy Bear is an articulated-jointed flatwood toy. The pivots allow the limbs to be bent. Bengee is made from multicore plywood, and the project involves fretting, riveting, and varnishing techniques.

Uncle Sam Banker Bear is an automaton money box. When the lever is pushed down, the coin falls through the slot and Uncle Sam Bear raises his hat and nods his head.

Roly-Poly is a turned rattle or shaker—a nice comfort toy for a baby or toddler.

Button and Buddy, the Bowling Bears, are a gravity-driven, somersaulting, topsy-turvy toy. The bears roll over and over and slowly travel down the parallel bar frame.

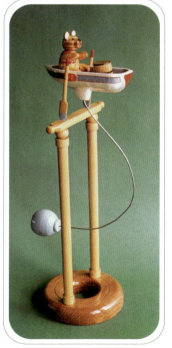

Barnacle Boatman Bear is a counterbalance desk-top toy. The boat can be "magically" balanced on the tips of the oars and rocked backward and forward.

The teddy truckers toy is a push-along truck with Crosley 1940 imagery and six peg-fit teddy bears.

Alan the Aviator Bear is a push-along toy plane with a flip-around propeller and a removable twist-and-lift teddy bear pilot.

This toy car is a likeness of a Cadillac 1959 Fleetwood Special. The bear has a crank-operated, side-to-side head movement.

Now, one piece at a time, hold the limb in one hand so that the end to be worked is pointing away from you. Then use the knife to slice away the waste, working with short, thumb-braced strokes, all the while cutting away from the hand that is holding the wood. Slice away the curve on one side; then turn the work over and slice away the curve on the other side.

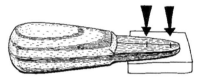

Continue turning the wood this way and that and removing more and more waste until you have achieved the 1-inch-long, ¼-inch-wide, flat-faced pivot-and-string area. When you have worked one limb, repeat the procedure with the others until all four limbs look more or less the same.

Run a pencil centerline down the flat face on all four limb turnings. Also make two marks, one ¼ inch along from the end for the pull-string hole, and another ⅝ inch along for the pivot-pin hole. Next, run the holes through with a ¹⁄₁₆-inch drill bit.

Study the working drawings to see how the pivot holes occur on the body at a point about ¼ inch in from the side edges; the leg holes are ¼ inch up from the bottom, and the arm holes are about 1 inch down from the top. Bear in mind that the holes need to be well-placed, and spike center points on the curved surface of the body. Then run the holes through with the ⅛-inch-diameter bit. The holes need to run through the front of the body, across the width of the limb slot, and on about ¼ inch into the back of the body.

Assembly

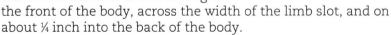

Cut four 10-inch lengths of twine or cord, and knot one length to each of the limbs. Make the knots as small as possible. Pull the knots into the string-pull holes, and make a secure fix with a drop of Super Glue.

When the glue is dry, slide the limbs, one at a time, in place in the body slot, and loosely pivot with the pins. Make sure that the four cords are placed so that they all come together between the two legs.

When you are happy with the fit and the working action, pencil label the limbs so that you know what goes where. Take the limbs out of the body, and move to the dust-free area that you have set aside for painting.

Painting & finishing

When you have rigged up a drying line, take the black acrylic paint and the fine-point brush and carefully paint in the small details that make up the design of the face. Give the bear a couple of coats of clear varnish, being sure to sand between coats and allow the paint to dry. Settle for a thin coat of varnish on moving mating surfaces (inside the slot and on the pivot areas).

Finally, put the bear back together. Punch the pins home so that the heads are below the surface. Top the nail holes off with small dabs of filler, and cover the filler with varnish. Knot on your chosen pull beads, and phew! Jolly Jumping-Jack Bear is ready and waiting for action!

Special tips

- If you have a large, powerful lathe you can skip the pre-lathe wood shaping and turn the wood down straight from a square section.
- If you are new to woodturning and are considering buying a special chuck, then you can't do better than a large, chunky, four-jaw chuck. The square-section wood can be mounted without any fussing about and, best of all, once the jaws are done up tight, the workpiece stays put.
- When you are choosing your wood, be sure to go for strong, straight-grained, knot-free varieties. In the context of teddy bears, we use American southern yellow pine because it has such an attractive toffee-twist color and texture.

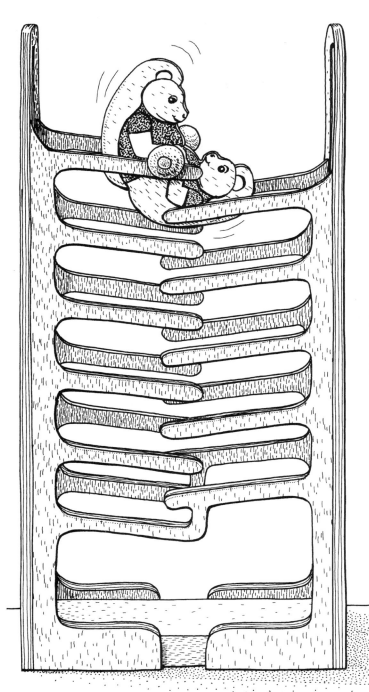

Button &
Buddy, the
bowling
bears

BUTTON AND BUDDY were having a wonderful roly-poly time. Forward, over and over, and . . . drop! Backward, over and over, and . . . drop! Over and over and over they roll, sometimes rolling down a slope and sometimes rolling up a slope, but always working their way down toward the bottom of the frame.

> Over and over and over they twirl
> One teddy boy and one teddy girl
> Two little roly-poly bears
> Rolling and bowling down the stairs!

> Roly-poly, down they go
> Sometimes fast and sometimes slow
> Just like going down the stairs
> Two little roly-poly bears!

Button and Buddy are a gravity-driven, somersaulting, topsy-turvy toy. The bears roll over and over and slowly travel down the parallel bar frame. This project utilizes a scroll saw and drill, multicore plywood, solid wood, as well as fretting, drilling, and color-staining techniques.

Materials   Best-quality birch multicore plywood, ¼ inch thick, 24"×24"
         (This allows for a generous amount of cutting waste.)
      4" length of ¼"-diameter dowel
      Two ¾"-diameter wooden beads, stained green
      8" length of prepared softwood, ¾" thick and 1⅞" wide, for the
         base block
      Handful of ½"-long panel pins or brads
      Super Glue (We used Loctite Super Glue 3.)
      Workout & tracing paper
      Watercolor inks in light green, red, & blue
      Black acrylic paint
      Clear, high-shine varnish
      Graded sandpapers

Tools   Small hammer
      Scroll saw
      Hand drill with a ¼"-diameter bit
      Pencil

Ruler
Compass
Try-square
Small, sharp-pointed craft knife or scalpel
Two soft-haired paintbrushes, broad & fine

Button and Buddy are really intriguing. Set them on the top of
the parallel-bar frame, give them a gentle push, and then
watch as they roll over and over, drop to the next level, climb
up the slope of the next parallel bars, change the direction of
spin, roll back down the bars, drop to the next level, and so
on—backward and forward, down toward the bottom of the
frame. Of course, sometimes they falter, and sometimes they
travel too fast and fall at a crooked angle, and sometimes you
have to give them another little push to set them on their way.
But mostly, if they are set on a level surface, they continue on
their momentous, gravity/antigravity journey.

Have a good, long look at the project picture, on page 62 and
the working drawing. The scale is 2 grid squares to 1 inch. The
parallel-bar frame stands 16 inches high, 7½ inches wide, and
2½ inches deep across the span of the bars.

Note how the length of the through-bear dowel and the placing
of the two wooden beads on the dowel are such that the
spinning bears are forced to run train-like along the parallel bar
"rails." Consider how the rolling momentum of the bears as
they spin downhill is enough to carry them up to the top of the
next hill before they then run out of energy and start to roll
backward down the next hill, and so on. See the way the four
plywood frames have been designed so that they can be run
through the scroll saw without the need for drilling saw-blade
starter holes.

The design is beautifully simple and direct. The line of cut runs
straight in at the bottom/top of the frame, around the various
shapes that make up the design, and then back out alongside
the entry cut. Best of all, the broad, generous curves make for
easy cutting.

Looking & planning

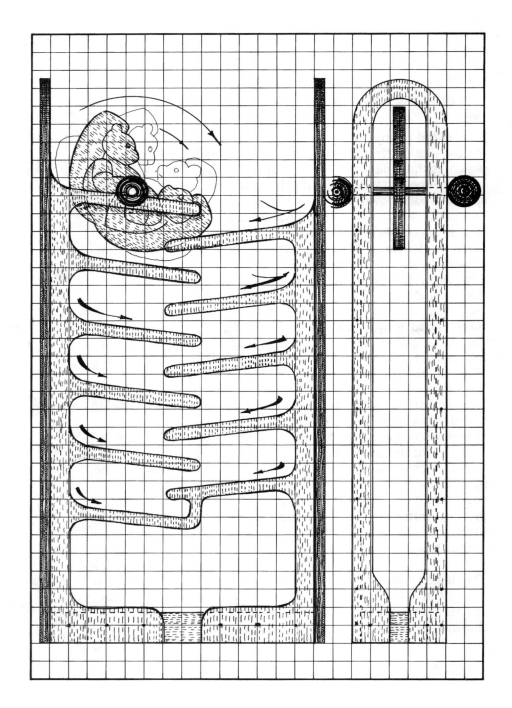

If you know how to use a scroll saw, then this project is going to be easy. That said, the initial setting out (drawing the design out on the wood and making sure everything is square and accurate) is more than a bit tricky.

Skill level

When you come to fretting out the wood, it's best to pin the sheets of ply together in pairs, and then cut them out two at a time. In this way, it is possible to achieve identical cutouts.

Study the project from every possible angle and consider how it needs to be set out, worked, and put together. Then use the pencil, ruler, compass, and square to draw the design up to full size, shown on page 64. From side to side of the frame, the paired bars need to be parallel and the same length, and the lines and curves need to be smooth rather than notched, so spend time making sure that the various forms are well set out. When you are happy that all is correct, take a clear tracing.

Setting out
the design

On the plywood, use the pencil, ruler, and square to draw out the overall rectangle shapes—the fronts and both sides of the frame. Have a ½-inch all-around margin of waste, shown on page 65. When you have drawn out the four sides, use the crosscut saw to swiftly slice them down to size. Put one front and one end board to one side.

This done, draw out the actual front and side frame sizes on the remaining boards. Make sure that they have straight sides and true 90° corners. The front frame needs to measure 7 inches wide and 13 inches high, and the curve-topped end should measure 2½ inches wide and 16 inches high. NOTE: All four rectangles must have straight sides and true 90° corners.

Now, using the carefully drawn-out rectangles as a framework guide, set about pencil-press transferring the traced designs through to the wood. Use a ruler and compass to rework the lines so that there is no doubting what goes where and how.

Having shaded in all the areas that need to be cut away, pair the boards with the guidelines uppermost—two fronts and two ends—and pin them together. Make sure that the pins are set on the positive or unshaded area (through the wood that makes

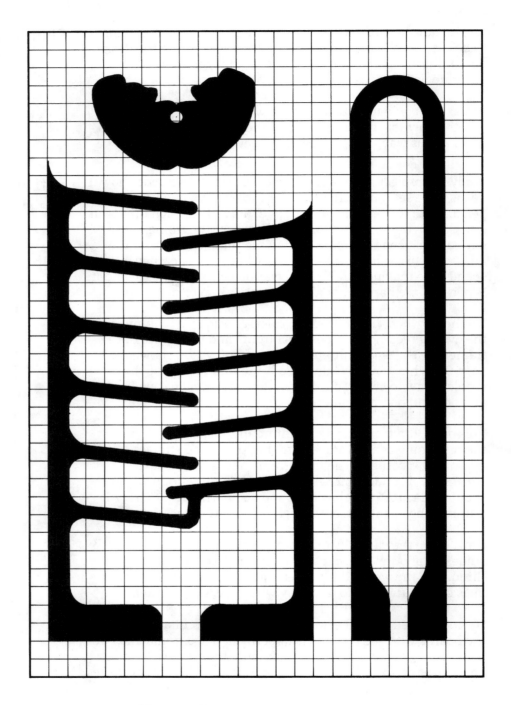

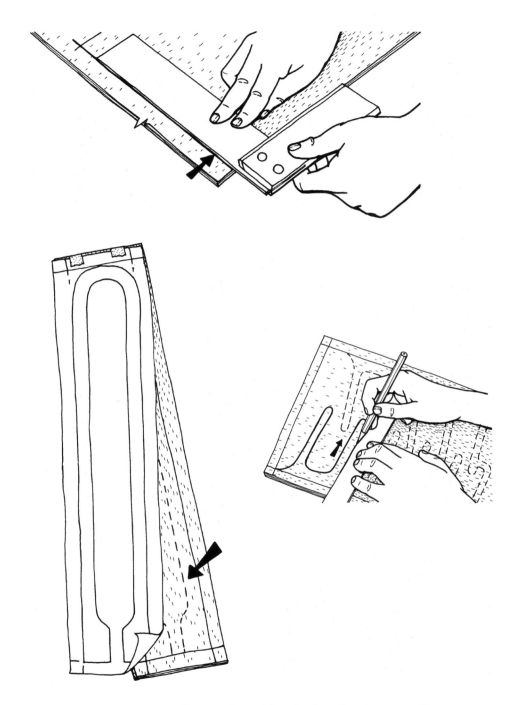

Button & Buddy, the bowling bears   65

up the frame) and leave the heads proud so that they are easy to remove.

Finally, take the tracing of the two bears and pencil-press transfer the design through to a single thickness of ¼-inch ply.

Fretting & fitting

When you are happy with the design, first use the straight saw to cut out the primary rectangles as shown, and then run the rectangles through the scroll saw. The procedure is easy and straightforward. All you do is start the cut on the bottom-of-frame edge, at the opening, and then gently feed the wood into the saw so that the line of cut is a little to the waste side of the drawn line.

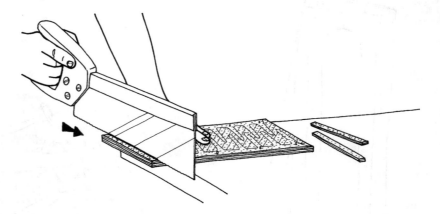

The key words when using the scroll saw are "nice and easy." That is to say you should go at a nice, easy pace—not so fast that the blade rips up the grain, nor so slow that the blade friction burns the wood or wanders off course. If you are at all unsure as to a good speed of cut, then it's best to have a tryout with some scrap wood. A good test of skill is to draw out half a dozen small, coin-sized circles and have a few practice runs until you can get it right.

Continue cutting out the curve-topped end profile, clearing the waste from the end-center and cutting out the rather complex front panels as shown. Certainly, it's a long slow job, but the good news is that if the blade is new and well-tensioned, and if

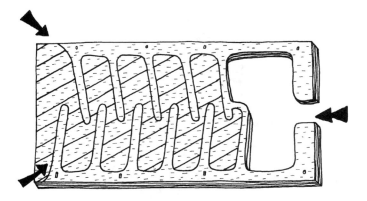

you work at a nice and steady pace, the workpiece should leave the saw with all the sawn edges being so smooth and clean-cut that they hardly need any sanding.

When you have cut out the ends, sides, and the bears, remove the pins, and ease the paired board apart. Swiftly rub all the cut edges down to remove any ragged grain.

When you have achieved the five cutouts, take the 8-inch length of prepared 1⅛-x-¾-inch section wood (the base block), and use the square to set it out at 7 inches long. Cut it to size and sand it to a smooth finish.

Next, glue and pin-fix the two 7-inch-wide plywood side profiles onto the edge of the base block. It's a good idea to use waste wood supports to check that the sides are at 90° and perfectly aligned.

Next, glue and pin-fix the curve-topped ends in place on the ends of the base block, dribble glue on mating faces, up the corners of the framework, and run pins through from the plywood ends and into the edges of the plywood front panels. Finally, fill the pinholes with wood filler, and rub the whole workpiece down to a smooth, clean-faced, round-cornered

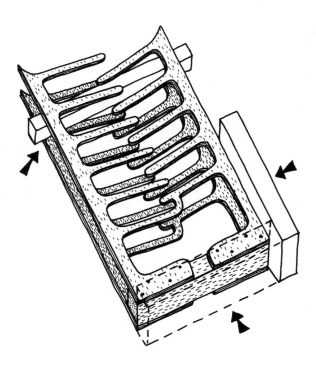

finish. NOTE: It's most important that the rails are round-topped in section, so check for unwanted ripples and dents.

Finishing & testing

Set the roly-poly bears cutout flat-down on the table, so that the pencil-drawn image is on the underside, and carefully slide it out over the edge of the table until it is nicely balanced. This done, hold the workpiece down while you run a pencil line along the table edge on the underside of the cutout.

Turn the cutout around approximately 90° on the spot, and repeat the procedure three or four times. If all is correct, when you flip the cutout over, the resultant intersection of all the drawn lines (the center of gravity) should be centered on the through-dowel point, as shown.

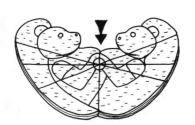

It's most important that the dowel center is at the center of gravity. If necessary, move the dowel point, adjust the imagery of the bears' hands accordingly, and rub out any unwanted lines. See to it that the bear imagery is transferred through to both sides of the wood. (See the painting grid on page 70 for the imagery.)

When you have established the center-of-gravity point of the two bears cutout, set the ¼-inch-diameter bit in the drill, and support the workpiece on a piece of scrap wood. Make sure that the hole is centered spot-on and check that the drill bit is at right angles to the face of the plywood; then run the hole through. Next, take the beads one at a time, hold them in a pair of rag-muffled grips and run the ¼-inch drill bit down through the thread hole. Take the 4 inch length of ¼-inch diameter dowel, slide it through the cutout hole and center it up, slide the beads on the ends of the dowel, and glue all three units in place with the Super Glue.

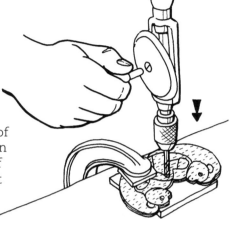

Now for the big test. Put the frame on a flat, level surface, set the bowling bears on the top rails, and give them a little starter push. If their downward journey is in any way jerky or halting, then either the rails are dented or the bears are off-balance. Both faults can be adjusted by careful sanding.

Study the project picture, shown on page 70 and see how the toy needs to be color-stained with water-based inks. Being careful to leave the base block natural, paint the frame light green, using the soft-haired brushes. When you come to the bears, paint one T-shirt red and the other blue. To stop the stain from bleeding, score in the design lines with the point of a scalpel around the T-shirts, as shown on page 70.

Color staining

When you are using colored inks, don't overload the brush and be sure to work well within the color areas as shown on page 70.

Next, take the fine-point brush and the black acrylic paint and carefully line-in the faces and the T-shirts. Wait awhile for the

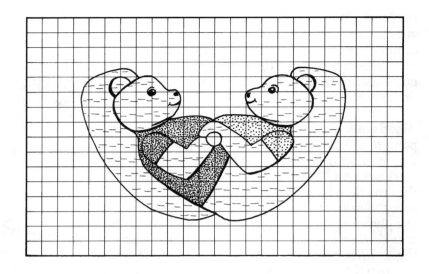

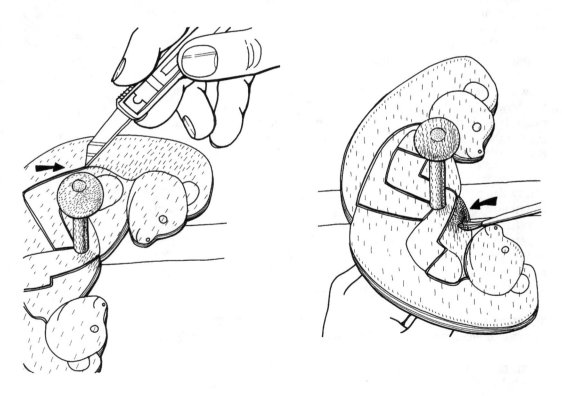

ink and the paint to dry, and then give the whole toy a thin coat of varnish—just enough to seal the wood.

When the sealer coat is dry, take the fine-grade sandpaper and rub all edges and surfaces down to remove the nibs. Make a really good job of the top edges of the runner rails, the sides of the bear spinner, and the dowel. Carefully wipe away the dust and give the whole toy a couple of coats of varnish. Put this aside to dry.

Finally, stand the frame on a level surface, set the bowling bears in place at the top of the frame, give them a little nudge, and watch them roll.

Special tips

- It's most important that the parallel bar side frames are identical. If they are badly matched or wobbly or notched, the spinner will get stuck, stop, or otherwise fail.
- For a perfect cut, the scroll saw blade needs to be new and well-tensioned. It's always a good idea to have a pack of spare blades at hand.
- The dowel must pass through the center of gravity or the balance point. If you don't get it right the first time around, then cut out another spinner and try again.
- In use, the toy must be set up on a smooth, level surface.

Larry the
Lumberjack Bear

LARRY THE LUMBERJACK

LARRY THE LUMBERJACK Bear was never so happy as when he was climbing trees. Of course, he liked singing, and dancing, and going to school, and swimming, and sleeping, and eating—he loved eating!—but best of all, he liked climbing trees.

Left, right, left, right . . . Larry climbed slowly to the top of the tree. And then, when the ropes went slack—Zip!—he slid back down again.

> Up and down, up and down, all day long!
> Climbing trees is such great fun
> I hardly ever stop
> Larry the Lumberjack is my name
> I'll climb right to the top!

> When Larry was up, he was up!
> When Larry was down, he was down!
> When Larry was only halfway up
> He was neither up nor down!

Larry is a traditional friction-climb toy. As the strings are pulled, the figure slowly climbs up the strings. This project uses a coping saw and a drill and involves the techniques of fretting, sanding, and painting on multicore plywood.

Materials

Best-quality birch-faced multicore plywood, ½" thick, 12"×12" (This size allows for mess-ups)
Couple of yards of smooth 1⁄16"-diameter cord or twine
Workout & tracing paper
Graded sandpapers
Acrylic paints in green, red, & black
Clear, high-shine varnish

Tools

Coping saw with a pack of spare blades to fit
Pencil
Ruler
Vise
Small hand drill with 1⁄16"-diameter bit
Small, hold-in-the-hand block of wood (for sanding)
Scissors
Paintbrushes, broad & fine

Larry the Lumberjack Bear draws his inspiration from a whole family of traditional climb-up-a-string toys. There are pirates and frogs and all manner of little spread-arm figures. In use, the cross-beam is hung from a hook, the strings are stretched taut and pulled in turn—left, right, left, right—and Larry slowly climbs up the strings toward the cross-beam. And, of course, as soon as the strings are slackened, he slides back down again. As to how and why the toy works, I think it has something to do with friction . . . but no matter! All you really need to know is that if you keep pulling the strings, Larry will keep on climbing.

Have a look at the project picture on page 73 and the working drawing on page 76. The scale is 4 grid squares to 1 inch. The bear measures about 4½ inches high and 4 inches wide across the span of the hands. Consider the angle of the through-hand cord holes, and the way the little cross-beam swivels up and down like a seesaw.

Study the design and consider possible modification—you could add beads, for example—and then draw the figure up to full size.

If you have a small workbench (a bench out in the garage or even a good, solid kitchen table), and if you have a coping saw, a vise, and a hand drill, this is a pretty straightforward and uncomplicated project. In fact this project is so easy, you could maybe consider it as a working-with-the-kids project. I would say that a keen 9- to 12-year-old could have Larry the Lumberjack cut out, drilled, painted, strung-up, and climbing in a morning. NOTE: If you or the kids are raw beginners, you are going to break blades! Be ready with a stack of spare coping saw blades.

When you have a clear understanding of just how the toy needs to be made, decorated, and put together, draw the design up to full size and make a tracing. When you are happy with the design, secure the tracing to the plywood with tabs of masking tape, and carefully pencil-press transfer the traced profile through to the wood.

Looking & planning

Skill level

Setting out & sanding

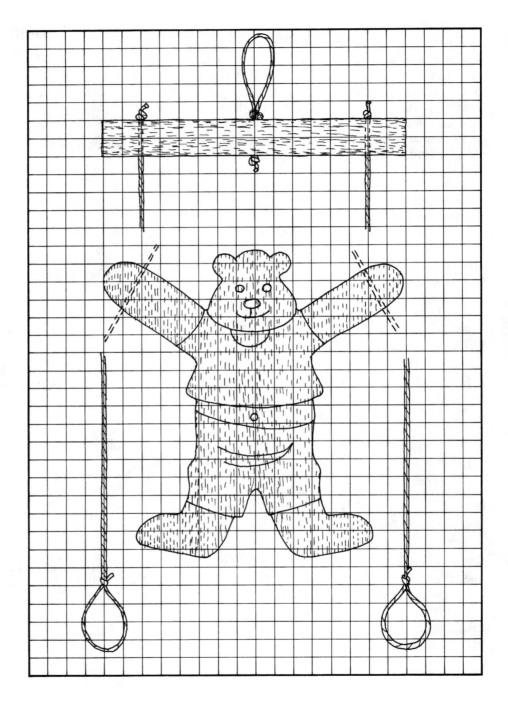

Draw in the through-hand cord lines. Having established a good clear profile line, clamp the wood in the vise and set to work with the coping saw, as shown. Work at a steady, easy pace, all the while keeping to the waste side of the drawn line, aiming for a cut edge that is clean and crisp.

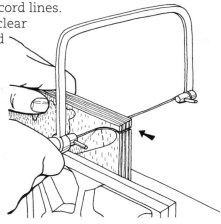

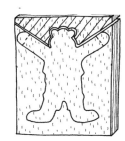

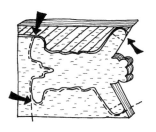

Maneuver both the wood and the tool so that the blade is always timely presented with the line of best cut. Finally, when you have fretted out the profile and the little cross-beam, support the graded sandpapers on a small block of wood, and rub the workpiece down to a smooth, slightly round-edged finish.

Fit the ⅟₁₆-inch-diameter bit in the drill, and secure the workpiece in the jaws of the vise. Align the drill with the angle of the cord hole, and run the hole from edge to edge through the width of the hand. Do this with both hand holes.

Drilling

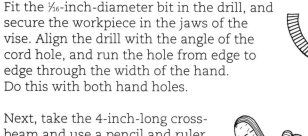

Next, take the 4-inch-long cross-beam and use a pencil and ruler to mark in the position of the three cord holes. Use the hand drill to bore out the three holes, one hole at center and the other two at about ½ inch from each end.

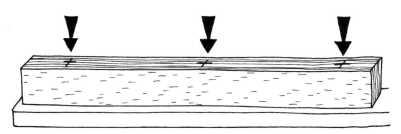

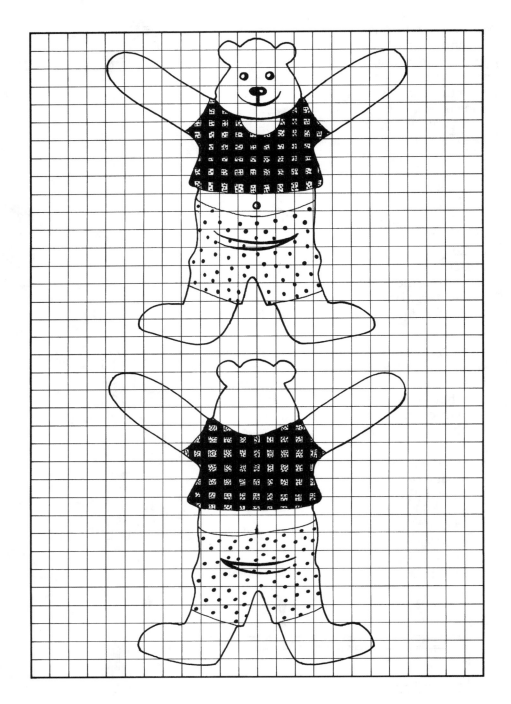

When you are happy with the placing of the various holes, pencil-press transfer the teddy bear imagery through to the profile (the trousers and the check shirt)—the front view on one side and the back view on the other. See the painting/color grid on page 78.

Start by clearing away the dust and debris and moving away to the area set aside for painting. Now, having stirred and mixed the acrylic colors, first lay on the ground colors: green for the trousers and red for the shirt.

Painting

Then, when the paint is dry, use the fine-point brush to pick out all the small details: the black criss-cross lines on the shirt, the crease-lines on the trousers, the tummy/belly button, the bottom lines, and the details of the face. When the acrylics are completely dry, give all surfaces a couple of coats of clear, high-shine varnish and put to one side to dry. You can use the hand holes to hang Larry up while he is being varnished.

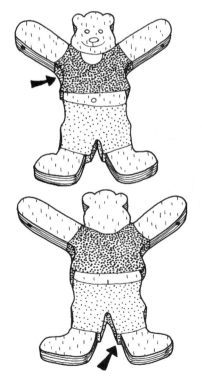

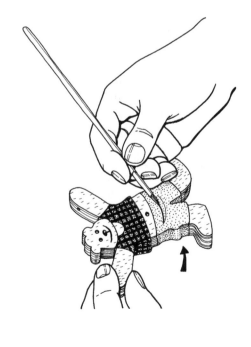

Assembly

When the varnish is dry, have a look at the string holes. If necessary, poke them through with a needle. Have another look at the working drawing, and start by looping about 8 inches of string through the center of the cross-beam and knotting on a hanging loop.

Next, cut two lengths of cord at about 30 inches for the two pull cords. It's very straightforward; one cord at a time, knot the pull cord at one end, pass it down through the cross-beam and on through the bear's arm hole, and tie off with a knot and/or loop. Do this with both cords.

Finally, dribble a drop of Super Glue onto all knots and Larry is ready for his first I'm-a-lumberjack-and-I-don't-care string-climbing adventure.

Special tips

- When you're ready to fit a new blade in the coping saw, have the teeth pointing away from the handle, and make sure that the blade is well-tensioned.
- When you are using the saw, hold it so that the blade, on its passage through the ply thickness, is at right angles to the working face.
- When you are drilling the through-hand cord holes, be extra careful that the drill is aligned. If necessary, ask a friend to help—one of you turning the handle while the other checks that angle of entry and exit are correct.
- By *hand drill,* we mean a plain and simple, hand-operated, cogged wheel, turn-and-push type drill (sometimes called an *eggbeater* drill). Such a tool is inexpensive, user-friendly, silent running, and altogether safe and easy to use. Be warned in this instance: When drilling into plywood edge grain, we do not recommend the use of an electric power drill. It's too swift and likely to run askew.

Betty Bear,
the nursery
clock

BIG COLORFUL balloons, twisty balloons, thin balloons, fat balloons, long balloons, and shiny pear-shaped balloons—Betty Bear loved them all. One day, she was given three of the biggest, brightest, and most beautiful balloons that you ever did see—one red, one yellow, and one green.

In fact, the balloons were so big that when she held on tight, Betty Bear started to float up into the sky. Up and up, higher and higher she floated, light as a feather. Her dress filled with air and billowed out wide until she looked like a balloon. Over the rooftops, over the hills, and over the sea. It was wonderful adventure. Betty Bear loved balloons!

> One, two, three balloons
> Floating in the sky
> Hold on Betty Bear
> It's time to go up high!
> Betty Bear can tell the time
> One, two, three
> Twelve o'clock is time for lunch
> And five's the time for tea

This nursery clock with Betty Bear and balloon imagery is a project that emphasizes fretting and piercing techniques.

Materials
Best-quality multicore plywood, ¼" thick, about 12"×12"
   (This allows a generous amount of cutting waste.)
2¾"-diameter clock face, with hands and a small battery-driven
   quartz clock mechanism to fit
Two picture screw-eye rings
36" length of thin, colored ribbon, yarn, or string
Tracing paper
Graded sandpapers
Acrylic paints in red, yellow, green, white, pale blue, & black
Clear, high-shine varnish

Tools
Coping saw or fretsaw with spare blades
Pencil
Ruler

Compass
Craft knife
Hand drill with ¼" drill bit
Soft-haired paintbrushes, fine & broad

Most of us, kids and adults alike, enjoy playing around with balloons. They are wonderfully ephemeral. One moment they are big, bold, and beautiful, and then the next—BANG! POW! WHOOSH! PISHHHH!—they are finished. And then again, there is something very special about the notion and concept of time. Tick, tick, tick . . . time passing, or as my dictionary so rightly says: "the continuous passage of existence in which events pass from a state of potentiality in the future, through to the present, to a state of finality in the past."

So what better than to bring together two delights—balloons and time—and present them in the form of a clock. Betty Bear the clock doesn't do more than tell the time, but for all that, she will brighten up your day. Hang Betty Bear on the wall in the kids' bedroom, and there she will be, hanging around, just waiting to tell you the time. A teddy bear that slowly drifts and sways in time to the soft tick-ticking—it's just got to be a good-fun idea.

Have a look at the working drawing on page 85 and the various details. The scale is 3 grid squares to 1 inch. Betty Bear stands about 6 inches high and 6 inches wide, while the balloons measure about 5 inches high and 8 inches wide. Consider how, with the bear suspended on strings or ribbons at about 12 inches long, the total clock length, from the top of the middle balloon down to the tip of the bear's toes, runs out at about 15 to 18 inches. Of course, if you want to lengthen the balloon ribbons, or have more balloons, or have the balloons much larger than the bear, or whatever, no problem. Simply adjust the details accordingly.

Note how the clock kit is no more than a metal/plastic face, a set of hands, and a little battery-operated quartz mechanism set in a small black plastic box. The face is fixed directly behind

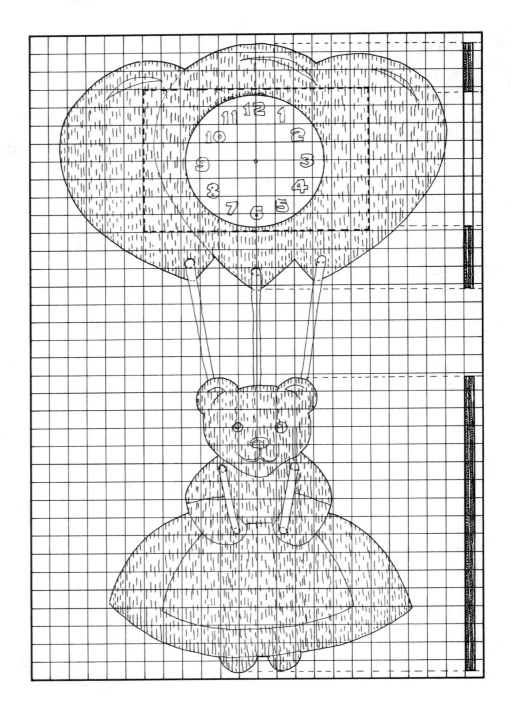

84   Teddy Bear Treasures

the 2¾-inch-diameter hole, and the black box is mounted on the back of the face.

This is a beautifully simple and direct project—just perfect for raw beginners to woodworking—in that it can be managed with a minimum of tools and expertise. A small amount of plywood, a coping saw, a drill, a small amount of fretting and painting, and you are two-parts finished.

And don't be put off by the idea of fixing the clock mechanism. The inexpensive and easy-to-fit clock kit can be fitted in the space of a few minutes. The face is mounted behind the hole and the black box is fitted at the back of the face—a few screws or an adhesive press-pad, and the job is done.

If necessary, modify the design to suit the size and shape of your clock kit. When you have gathered together all your tools and materials, draw the design up to full size, following the pattern provided on page 86. Make a tracing, and then carefully pencil-press transfer the traced lines through to your chosen sheet of plywood. At this stage, don't worry about the details of costume and face. Just make sure that the cutting lines (the edge profile and the hole for the clock face) and the position of the drilled holes are all crisply and clearly set out.

Next, with the wood held flat-down on a piece of waste, use the drill to run the holes through the ¼-inch ply thickness as shown on page 87. Cut eight holes in all—four through the teddy, one at the bottom of each of the three balloons, and a single saw-blade pilot hole set somewhere within the 2¾-inch-diameter circle of waste.

Having clearly established the line of cut, secure the wood in the vise and, with the coping or fretsaw, carefully cut out the bear and the balloon forms as shown on page 87. As you are working, try to hold the saw so that the cut edge stays at right angles to the working face. Aim to keep the cut edge smooth and crisp.

Finally, when you have fretted out the balloons, set them in the vise and unhitch the saw blade. Pass one end of the blade

Skill level

Setting out & fretting

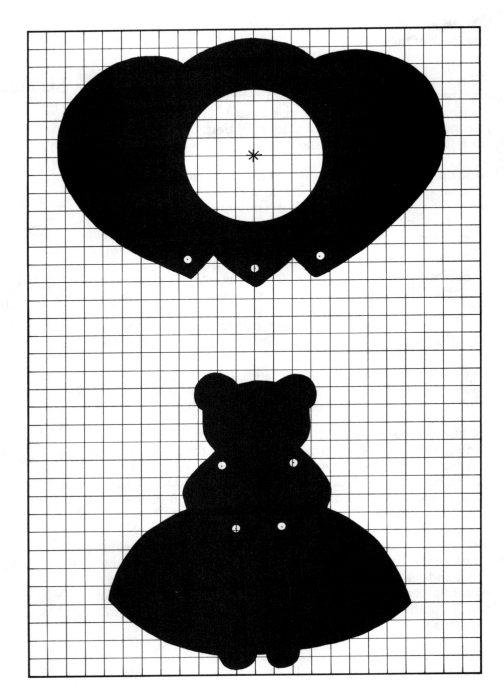

through the pilot hole, re-tension the blade, saw out the clock-face hole, and remove the saw.

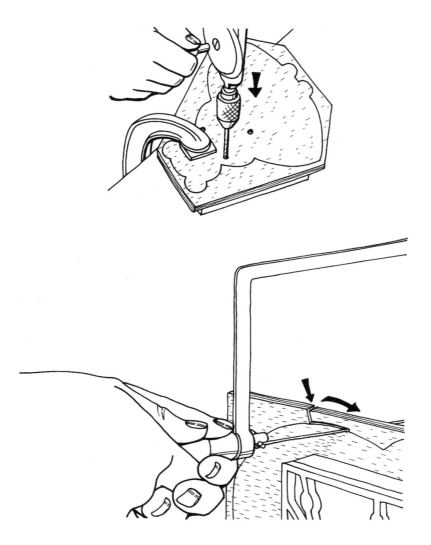

When you have fretted out the two forms, take a medium-grade sandpaper and rub the whole workpiece down to a smooth, slightly round-edged finish.

Painting & finishing

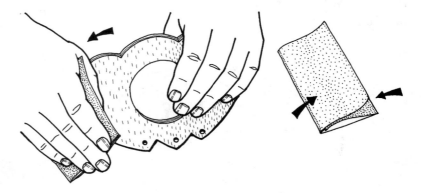

Go back to the tracings and carefully pencil-press transfer the imagery through to the best face of the bear and the balloons. Spend time getting it just right.

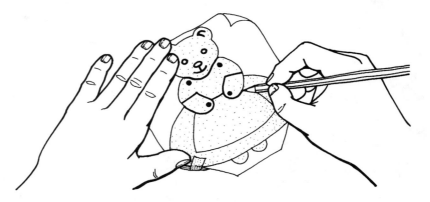

Study the painting grid on page 89, and establish all the lines that make up the design. Block in the forms with the acrylic paints. Try to keep all the painted edges smooth and even.

First define the edge of the area to be painted, and then block in the shape as shown on page 90. Paint one balloon red, one yellow, and one green. Paint the bear's frock blue and her apron white.

When the large areas of color are dry, use the fine-point brush to paint in all the details as shown on page 90—the white highlights on the balloons, the black details of the face, and so

Betty Bear, the nursery clock   89

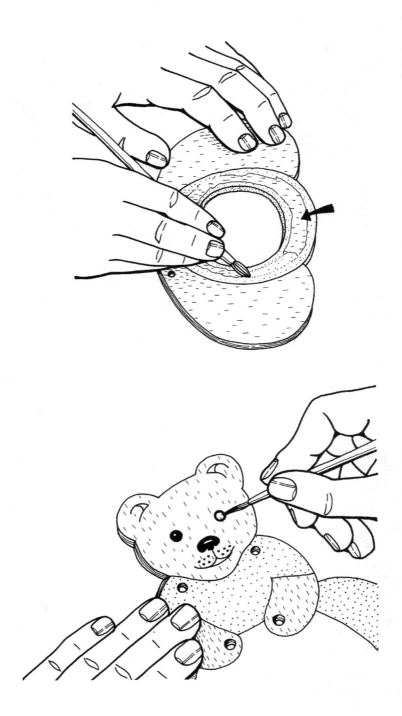

on. When you are happy that all is correct, allow the acrylic paints to dry completely. Not forgetting to sand between coats, give the whole workpiece a couple of generous coats of clear varnish and put it to one side to dry out.

When the varnish is dry, screw-fit the two screw-eye rings and hang the balloons-clock on the wall. Next fit-and-knot the three ribbons or cords so that the clock hangs straight. It's best to have the middle ribbon slightly slack so that the two side ribbons take the weight.

Finally, align and fit the face behind the clock-face hole. Mount the mechanism behind the face, and fit the hands, and Betty Bear is always ready and waiting to give you the time of day!

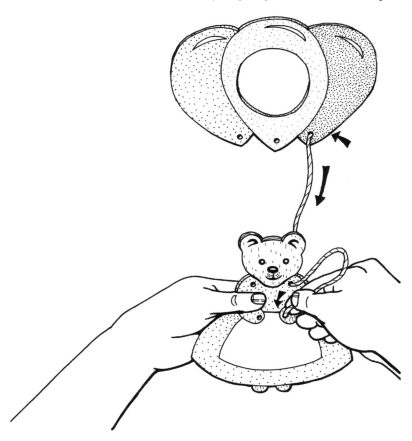

Betty Bear, the nursery clock **91**

Special tips

- Make sure that you use best-quality plywood.
- If the cut edges look in any way to be crumbly or there are cavities, then use a small amount of two-tube filler to make good the defects.
- If you decide to speed up the project by using an electric scroll saw, be sure to work at a steady, easy pace so as not to tear the grain of the wood. Have a trial run with a piece of scrap wood.
- There are many types of clock kits, some with contact-adhesive pressure-pad fixings, others with screw fixing, others with bolts and clips, and so on. It's best to read the instructions prior to the project, and then maybe to adjust the working methods and/or materials to suit.

Alan the Aviator Bear

ALAN THE AVIATOR

Bear hummed a little song to himself as he climbed into the cockpit of his 1940s American Thunderbolt stunt-fighter flyer. He buckled on his flying helmet, settled himself snugly down into the cockpit, and pressed the ignition button. The prop started to spin. Brrrum, brrum, brrum! He checked through the controls, and then gently pulled the joystick. The plane climbed higher and higher up into the clouds.

"Wonderful! Here we go!" he laughed, as he threw the plane into a spin and skimmed and hedge-hopped the little plane across the rooftops. Alan was so happy he sang another little song!

> Here I am in my plane,
> Brrrrrum brrrum broooom
> Ready to take off again
> Zoom zoom zoom!

> Here I am in the sky
> Zoom, zoom, zoom
> Don't you wish that you were I?
> Brrum brrum brrum!

This project is a push-along toy plane with a flip-around propeller and a removable twist-and-lift teddy bear pilot. It involves the use of a lathe, straight saw, scroll saw, chisel, knife, and drill. You will use lime, jelutong, and multicore plywood and practice turning, fretting, whittling, and painting.

Materials

Best-quality white-faced multicore plywood, ¼" thick, 18"×18", for the wings, wheels, and undercarriage (This allows for a good amount of spare for cutting waste and mistakes.)

16" length of easy-to-turn square section wood, 3"×3", for the fuselage

20" length of easy-to-turn strongly grained wood, 2"×2" square section for the teddy bear pilot (We used American southern yellow pine.)

8" length of easy-to-carve wood, 2"×1" section, for the propeller (We used lime.)

Nine brass round- or dome-head screws for the fixings (8 small
   and 1 large one for the prop) with washers to fit
5" length of ¼" dowel for the wheel pivots, the head-body peg, &
   the cockpit location peg
White PVA wood glue
Workout & tracing paper
Package of panel pins or brads
Graded sandpapers
Matte acrylic paints in colors to suit (We used red, yellow,
   black, & white.)
Small can of clear, high-shine varnish

Workbench with a vise.
Pencil
Ruler
Woodturning lathe with a four-jaw chuck to fit
Selection of turning tools
Compass
Dividers
Calipers
Straight saw
Coping saw
1"-wide flat chisel
Small knife for whittling
Electric scroll saw (We used a Hegner.)
Pillar drill with bits at 1¾", ⁵⁄₁₆" & ¼"
Long-nosed pliers
Soft-haired paintbrushes, fine & broad

This teddy bear in an airplane is a beautiful toy, a real delight
for children and adults alike. The bright red body of the plane,
the brilliant yellow go-faster flashes on the wings, the flip-
around propeller, the black wheels, and Alan the Teddy Bear
Aviator all make for a fun, sturdy, action toy. It's the perfect
plaything for small love-to-crawl-around-on-the-floor kiddies—
small children who want no more than a toy they can push and
zoom around the carpet.

Have a look at the working drawings on page 96 and 97. The
scale is 2 grid squares to 1 inch. The plane is about 12 inches
long from nose to tail, 16 inches across the span of the wings,

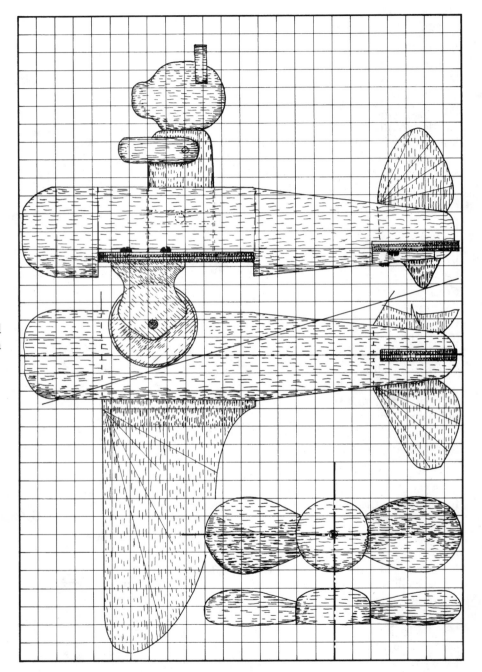

Scale: 2 grid
squares=1 inch

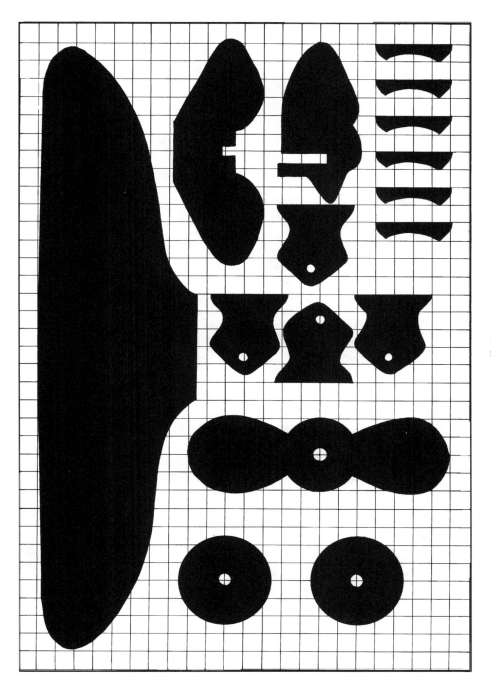

Scale: 2 grid squares=1 inch

Alan the Aviator Bear   97

and 9-10 inches high from ground level to the top of the teddy's ears.

Note the way the wings are variously slotted and let into the body of the fuselage. Consider how the toy is made up from a combination of solid wood and best-quality multicore plywood—with the fuselage and the propeller being made from lime, the teddy from strong-grained American southern yellow pine, and all the flat parts from plywood.

Have a close look at the details of the bear shown on page 96. See how his grooved body and the through-fuselage pin allows him to be loosely pivoted and located in the cockpit.

Consider well all the technique implications of making a toy of this size, type, and character. For example, have you got a medium-size lathe? Do you have a good large drill bit for the cockpit hole? Do you enjoy turning, scroll saw work, and whittling? All such points need to be well considered before you put tools to wood. Before you start, take note of the tools, techniques and materials, and decide whether or not you want to work through the project as suggested or make modifications.

Skill level

This is the perfect project for keen, multiskilled woodworkers. It's one of those projects that, on the face of it, looks much more complicated than it really is. Certainly the turning can be tricky, and, yes, whittling the propeller calls for a deal of patience. But for all that, the techniques are relatively uncomplicated and straightforward.

What else to say, except to emphasize that it's always good, sound working practice at the onset of a project to spend plenty of time checking through the working drawings and generally familiarizing yourself with all the details.

Turning the fuselage

Having studied the working drawings and design templates, take the length of 3-x-3-inch-square section wood and check it over to make sure that it is free from easy-to-spot flaws like loose, dead knots and grain splits. If you aren't too sure just how your chosen wood type is going to behave, it's best go

ahead anyway and mark any resultant problems down to
experience.

Set the section ends out with crossed diagonals and establish
the end centers. Having checked your lathe over to make sure
that it is in good working order, and having read through the
pre-switch-on safety list (see Glossary), set the wood in the
four-jaw chuck. Draw up the tailstock center and make sure
that the wood is secure. Then position the tool rest and switch
on the power.

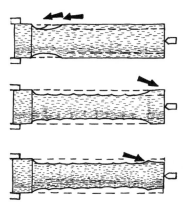

With the round-nosed gouge, work swiftly from left to right
along the spinning wood and remove all the waste. When you
have a roughed out cylinder, set the calipers to 2½ inches.

Now, take the tool of your choice (we used a skew chisel) and
turn the wood down to a smooth 2½-inch-diameter cylinder.
Use the calipers to make diameter checks, as shown.

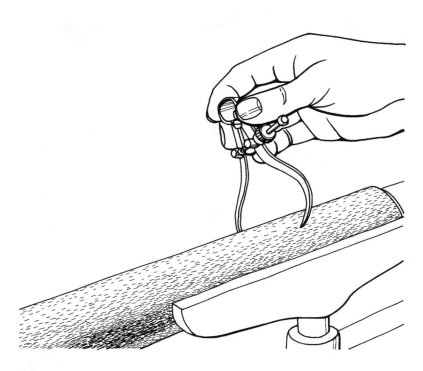

Next, take the dividers and the ruler and set the cylinder out from left to right, with all the stepoffs that go to make up the design. Working from the tail through to the nose of the plane, allow:

- a small amount for chuck waste
- ¾ inch
- 1⅝ inches
- 3 inches
- 4½ inches
- ¾ inch
- 1½ inches
- a final 2 inches for tailstock waste

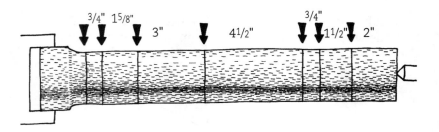

Note that some of the stepoff marks are no more or less than registration marks that are used at a later stage to fix the position of the wings. With the wood spinning, use either the points of the dividers or the point of the skew chisel, to score the stepoff marks into the face of the wood.

Having familiarized yourself with the long, round-ended cigar shape of the fuselage, take the round-nosed gouge or the skew chisel, and turn the wood down to the envisaged shape. As you are turning down the waste, keep one eye on the working drawings and design templates, and the other eye on the spinning wood, all the while trying to visualize the shape of the fuselage.

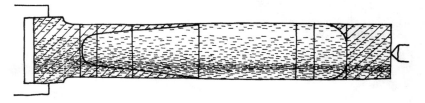

Using the marked stepoffs as a guide, turn the central long, straight section for the wing seating and the cockpit, the taper down to the tail, and finally the beautiful round nose. Continue by variously reducing, shaping, smoothing, and curve-cutting, until you have what you consider is a good, clean, well-considered form.

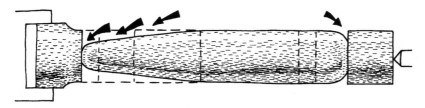

Finally, give the spinning wood a swift rubdown with the graded sandpaper, and finalize the rounded ends as you part off.

Turning the teddy

Study the teddy working drawing shown on page 102. Take the 20-inch length of 2-x-2-inch-square section wood and fix the end centers by drawing in crossed diagonals. Secure the wood in the four-jaw chuck, draw up the tailstock center, position the tool rest, and switch on the power.

Start by swiftly turning the wood down to a 2-inch-diameter cylinder. When you have achieved the smooth cylinder, use the pencil, ruler, and dividers to mark the wood from left to right with all the stepoffs that go to make up the design. Examine the illustration on page 103, and allow the following:

- 1½ inches for chuck waste
- 3 inches for the body
- 1 inch for waste
- 2½ inches for the head
- 1 inch for waste
- 2 inches for one arm
- 1 inch for waste
- 2 inches for the other arm
- another 1 inch for waste
- ¼ inch for each of the two ears, with a small amount of waste in between
- the rest of the length for waste and repeats

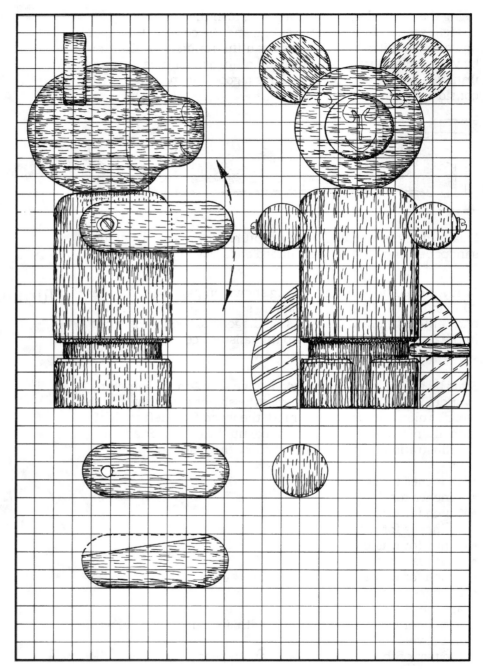

Scale: 2 grid
squares=1 inch

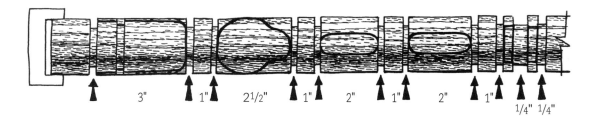

3"   1"   2½"   1"   2"   1"   2"   1"

¼" ¼"

Turning and forming the body is simple enough. Just turn the body section down to a smooth 1⅝-inch-diameter cylinder, and then round off the shoulders with the skew chisel. Sink the pivot groove with the parting tool. Figure on having the pivot groove about ³⁄₁₆ inch deep and set about ¾ inch up from the base.

When you come to turning the shape of the head, don't try too hard to follow any carefully marked-off form, but simply turn off the shape by eye. Having allowed for waste between the end of the body and the start of the back of the head (the helmet end) mark in about 1¾ inches for the helmet and round off the back.

This done, reduce the diameter of the cylinder between the helmet/face and the end of the bear's nose—turn it down to about 1 inch diameter—and then use the skew chisel to further turn the wood down until you achieve the bear's friendly round nose. Don't worry too much if the head shape is slightly shorter or a bit fatter or whatever. Such details make for "bear character."

Reduce the diameter around the arms/ears area. Continue, turning the two sausage shapes for the arms and the two cylinders for the ears.

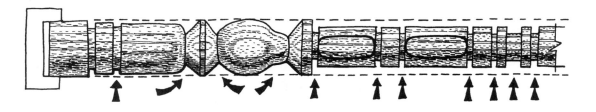

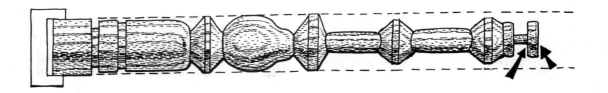

When you are happy with the string of turnings, give the work a swift rub-down with the sandpapers and, working along from the ears as shown, part off from the lathe.

Assembly

Having removed the turned components from the lathe, take a scrap of sandpaper and rub the part-off points down to a good finish. Swiftly rub the base of the body turning down to a level finish, and mark in the top center point. Now take the ¼-inch drill and run a straight hole down into the neck of the turning.

This done, run a pencil line down at front center, from the turned groove down through to the base. Take the tool of your choice—you might use a narrow chisel or a small penknife—and carefully whittle and pare a straight, clean-cut channel down from the around-the-body groove and on through to the base. While you have the knife at hand, slice away the flat area of waste on the body side of the arms.

Fitting the teddy bear's ears is more than a little bit difficult, so be warned and take it easy. First mark in on the head turning the position of the neck, the eyes, the nose, and, of course, the two ears. Make sure that the strong lines of the grain run parallel and level with what will be the base or horizon line. When you are happy with the placing of all the details, drill the hole in the bottom of the head for the neck dowel.

Bearing in mind that the ear discs are ¼ inch thick and about 1 inch in diameter, use the saw and the chisel to scoop out the two little part-disc holes. Best to mark the two ears "left" and "right," and then to cut each hole to fit, having defined the width of the slots with the saw.

Support the head in one hand and the chisel in the other, and remove the waste with a series of little scoops. Having cut the slots and trimmed the ear discs to a good fit and carefully noted how you want the grain of the ears to run in relationship to the head, smear glue on mating surfaces. Then set the ears in their slots and put this to one side until the glue is set. Finally, glue and dowel-fix the head to the body, and the bear is finished.

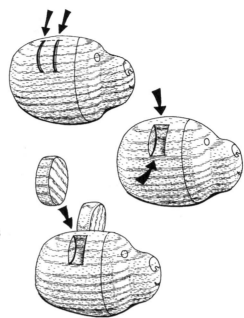

Cutting the plywood shapes

There are 17 plywood cutouts in all: a main through-wing, a tail through-wing, a rudder, four undercarriage side plates, six distance pieces and four circles that go to make up the two ½-inch-thick wheels. Trace these pieces off the design template shown on page 97, and pencil-press transfer the traced shapes through to the plywood.

Switch on the scroll saw, and very swiftly cut the wood down to easy-to-handle pieces. Now, take the single cutouts—the wings and the rudder—and set to work carefully fretting out the drawn shapes.

Using the scroll saw is simple enough, as long as you go at a nice and easy pace, all the while making sure that the line of cut is a little to the waste side of the drawn line. Pay particular attention to the symmetry of the wings and the fit of the slots. Finally, rub all the cutouts down to a smooth-faced, slightly round-edged finish.

Fitting the wings

Have a look at the working drawing on page 96 and see how the tail rudder and wings are slotted together and then slotted and bedded into the tail end of the fuselage. Note the way the fuselage has been cut to provide a level seating for the main through wing. See also how the cockpit hole goes right through the fuselage, with the wing covering the open bottom of the cockpit hole.

Having established the position of the leading and tail edges of the wing on the fuselage, support the fuselage in the jaws of a muffled vise and run saw cuts down into the wood to a depth of about ¾ inch. Try to keep the saw cuts square with the face of the wood (that is, with the axis of the turning).

Next take the straight chisel and carefully lower the wood between the cuts to a depth of ¾ inch to make a smooth, flat, level seating for the main wing. Chop at an angle into the initial saw cuts, and then remove the resultant peak of waste as shown on page 107. Work from side to center, all the while being extra careful not to split the wood as the chisel exits from a cut. Aim for a wedge-tight fit. Repeat the procedure for the back wings.

Fitting the rudder is a little more complicated because it has to slot into both the back wings and the round end of the fuselage. Mark in the position of the rudder, and then use the coping saw to cut away the waste. Start by cutting the slot a bit too small, and then gradually—with saw, chisel, and sandpaper—work toward a good fit.

When you are happy with the fit of the wings and rudder, put them to one side, and use the measure, pencil, and dividers to fix the position of the cockpit. Bearing in mind how important it is that the cockpit bore hole be well placed and vertical, take

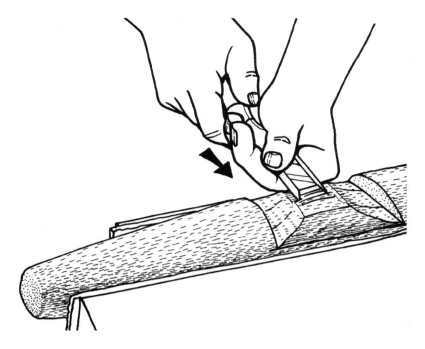

the drill and the 1¾-inch bit and run a hole from top side, down to the wing seating, right though the fuselage turning. Best to support the exit face with a piece of scrap wood so that the bit doesn't break through in a rush and tear the wood. Have the scrap wood running across the fuselage, flat against the wing seating.

While you have the drill out and having established the precise placing of the hole, run the ¼-inch-diameter bit from the side of the fuselage on through to the cockpit for the hold-bear-in-place dowel. Finally, rub the edges of the cockpit hole down to a smooth, slightly round-edged finish.

Each wheel support is made up from five thicknesses of ¼-inch-thick ply (two side plates and three spacers), and each of the wheels is made up from two thicknesses. Set the rough cutouts in stacks, with a pattern piece uppermost, and pin them together, placing the pins or brads inside the pattern area, as shown. Make sure that the heads are well proud, and that the points go no more than about halfway through the bottom thickness.

Landing gear & wheels

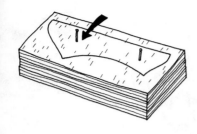

Establish the position of the axle holes in the wheels and run them through with the ⁵⁄₁₆-inch drill bit. Repeat the procedure with the undercarriage side plates, only this time have the holes slightly smaller, at ¼ inch.

Now, with the holes drilled and the various ply layers still pinned together, set to work with the scroll saw and cut out the shapes. Have the saw blade well tensioned to avoid the blade drifting, and see to it that the line of cut runs a little to the waste side of the drawn line. When you come to cutting the wheels, try to cut a really good, smooth curve.

Remove all the pins with the long-nosed grips, sand the edges, and group the various cutouts so as to make the two-wheeled landing gear units. When you are happy with the arrangement, smear glue on all mating surfaces and clamp up.

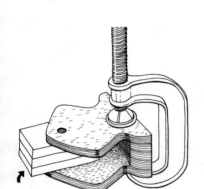

When the glue is dry, rub the components down with the graded sandpaper until all the sawn faces are smooth and slightly round-edged. Having marked in the position of the wheel supports on the underside of the wing, run two small holes through the wing thickness and have a trial fitting.

Finally, fit the two wheels on the screw chuck, secure the chuck on the lathe, then switch on the power and use sandpaper to rub the wheels down to a smooth-edged finish.

Whittling the propeller

Take the 8-inch length of 2-x-1-inch section wood and set it flat down on the bench so that the 8-x-2-inch face is uppermost. Fix the center-point by drawing in two crossed diagonals. Now, having first used the crossed diagonals and the center point to fix the position of both the vertical and horizontal axis, take a tracing from the design template and pencil-press transfer the bow-tie shape of the propeller through to the wood.

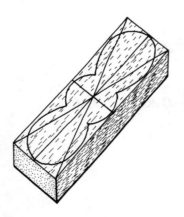

Remove the workpiece to the scroll saw, and cut out the basic bow-tie form. Set the cutout flat down on the worksurface, so that the 7-inch-long shape is aligned horizontally. Draw in the central circle or boss, and shade in the bottom left and the top right quarters of the prop blades. Then flip the wood over and repeat the procedure on the other side.

When you are ready to start whittling, first support the workpiece on the bench and define the edge of the boss with a ⅛-inch-deep straight-down stop cut. Then clasp the workpiece dagger-like in your left hand, so that the area to be worked is pointing toward you. Now take the knife in your right hand, and clear away the waste on the bottom right-hand quarter nearest you.

Work a series of small, tight, thumb-paring cuts, all the while whittling from boss center to end and lowering the waste on the 3- to 6-o'clock quarter. The best way to achieve a nicely balanced overall form is to keep the workpiece turning end to end and side to side, all the while redefining the boss and lowering, shaping, and otherwise working the 3- to 6-o'clock quarter. When you have what you consider is a good form, rub the whole workpiece down with the graded sandpapers until all faces and edges are smooth and rounded to the touch. Finally, run a ¼-inch-diameter hole through the center of the boss.

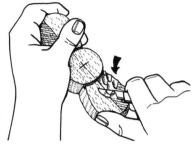

With a toy of this character, it's best to paint the components before you put them together. Have a look at the various drawings and, especially, the painting grid on page 110. See how the fuselage is painted bright red, the wings yellow with red flashes, the pilot's face details and helmet black, the undercarriage red, and so on.

That said, if you decide to go for different colors, no problem. You just modify the order of work accordingly.

Having made good with filler and sanded the wood smooth, remove the various components to a clean, dust-free area that you have set aside for painting, and arrange all your paints and materials so that they are comfortably to hand. Rig up a pin, string, and cotton drying line, so that you can string up the components once you paint them.

Lay the matte acrylic paints on in smooth, thin, even coats, all the while making sure that you brush out any runs and smears, and lightly sandpaper between coats. Lay on at least a couple of coats.

Painting & assembly

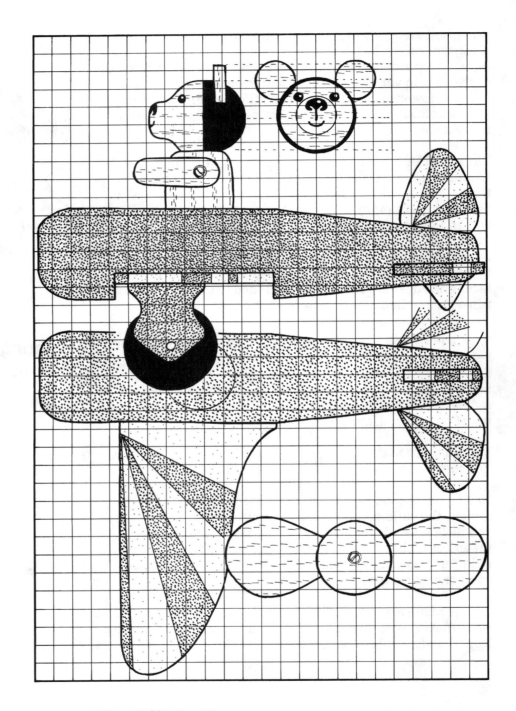

When the ground colors are dry, pencil in the design details, define the edges with a fine-point brush, and then use a large brush to block in the enclosed areas.

When the various parts are well painted and completely dry, then comes the really pleasuresome task of putting the toy together. Having made sure that all the finish is good and all holes correctly placed, start by fitting the wheels.

Cut two 1½-inch lengths of ¼-inch-diameter dowel and round over the ends with sandpaper. Position a wheel and washers between the undercarriage side plates, and tap the dowel into place. If all is well, the dowel should be a tight fit in the plate holes and a loose, easy-run fit through the wheels. Do this with both wheels.

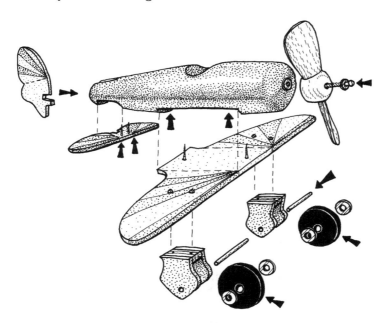

Now, having carefully established the position of the landing gear on the underside of the main wing, fit and fix them in place with brass round-head screws. Next, slide the wing into its seating, making sure that it is symmetrical and well aligned, and screw it into place. The same goes for the back wings and rudder—ease them into place, make sure they are aligned, and fit with brass screws.

Now, not forgetting to have washers between all moving parts, run a good, long, fat brass round- or dome-head screw through the propeller boss, and screw the propeller to the nose of the plane. You might at this stage need to touch up any scuffs or grazes with paint.

When the touch-ups are dry, hang the plane and the pilot from cotton threads, and give the whole toy several coats of clear varnish. Rub down slightly between coats, and be careful not lay on so much varnish that moving parts stick together, or that the cockpit becomes too tight a fit for the pilot. Finally, pop Alan the Aviator into his cockpit seat, turn him to face front so that he stays put, and he is ready for his first dare-devil loop-the-loop.

Special tips

- When you choose your wood for the fuselage, make sure that you use an easy-to-turn type that is straight-grained and free from knots.
- If you only have a small lathe, the teddy's head and body can be turned from one length, and the arms and ears from another length
- If you find that some of the cut ply edges are gappy, fill with two-tube resin filler.
- If you decide to use wood types and/or paints other than those described, make sure that they are completely safe and non-toxic.
- If you have a selection of plywood thicknesses left over from other projects, you could use ½-inch-thick ply for the wheels, ¾-inch-thick ply for the landing gear spacers, and so on.
- If you are at all unsure about any part of the project, it's always a good idea to sort out the problems by making a prototype from scrap wood.
- Make sure that Alan Bear's body is an easy, loose fit in the cockpit. Allow for paint and varnish build-up. Note that, after painting and varnishing, the body gets slightly fatter and the cockpit hole gets slightly narrower.

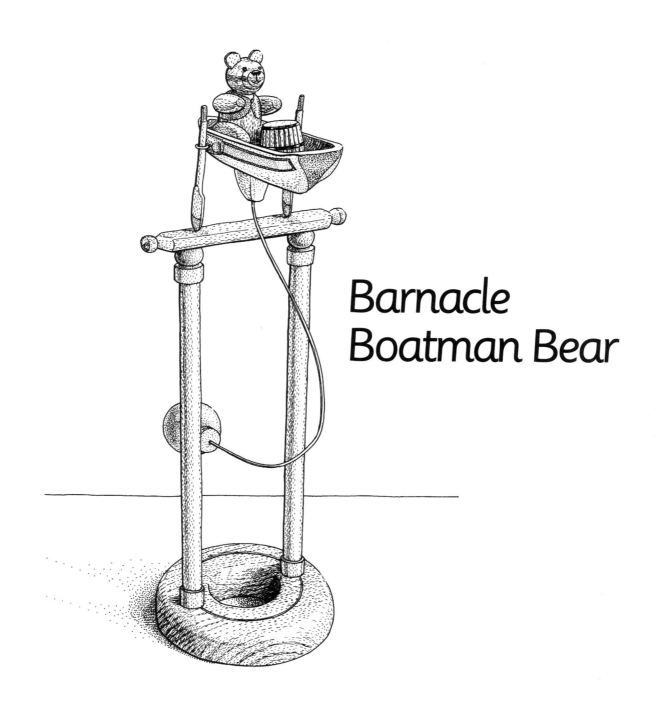

Barnacle
Boatman Bear

BARNACLE BOATMAN Bear loved messing about in his little rowboat—the sun, the sea, the sand, and lots and lots of water—what a wonderful life! He carefully set the barrel of soda pop down in the boat, seated himself comfortably, slid the oars in the rowlocks, and then started to row.

Dip, heave, pull, splash. Dip, heave, pull, splash. The little boat rocked and bobbed across the water. Barnacle Bear was having a good-fun time. He was soaking wet, his arms ached, and he was feeling very thirsty. He looked at the barrel of soda pop . . . Mmmm!

> Barnacle Bear rows his boat
> Across the wide blue sea
> Up and down . . . Up and down
> As free, as free can be!
>
> Dip and pull . . . Dip and pull
> In a boat so new and shiny
> Dip and pull . . . Dip and pull
> Across the great blue briny.

Barnacle Boatman Bear is a counterbalance desktop toy. The boat can be "magically" balanced on the tips of the oars and rocked backward and forward.

Materials

6" length of prepared easy-to-carve wood, 2½" wide, 1½" thick, for the rowboat (Best to use a wood like jelutong or lime/linden.)

6½"-square slab of heavy, easy-to-turn wood, 2" thick, for the base (We used elm, but you could just as well use oak, beech, or maple.)

14" length of 1¾"×1¾"-square section wood for the bear (We used American southern yellow pine.)

Jelutong

    33" length, 1¼"×1¼"-square section wood for the two dowel uprights

    12" length of 1"×½" section for the cross-beam (This allows for a generous amount of end waste.)

Odds and ends for the oars, keel block, rowlock mounts, counterbalance ball, and the seat
24" coat-hanger wire for the counterbalance arm (This allows for waste.)
Workout & tracing paper
Two brass screw-eyes to fit the ¼"-diameter oar
Four 1"-long pins/brads for fixing the stand
Super Glue
Masking tape
Graded sandpapers
Acrylic paint in red, white, blue, & black
Clear, high-shine varnish

Electric scroll saw with a 3" cut and a pack of heavy-duty blades to fit
Lathe with a four-jaw chuck and a 6"-diameter face plate to fit
Set of woodturning tools
Dividers
Calipers
Pencil
Ruler
Try-square
Bench drill with a good selection of bits
Wood carver's spoon gouge, for scooping out the inside of the boat
A couple of sharp whittling knives (We used a broad-blade penknife for the heavy work and a scalpel for the small details.)
Small saw for cutting the ear slots
Small hammer
Pliers or grips for bending the wire
Workbench with a vise
Soft-haired paintbrushes, broad & fine

Barnacle Boatman Bear draws his inspiration from an Edwardian desktop counterbalance toy. We saw it in an old English arts and crafts magazine dated about 1920. This toy is a real delight. Set it in pride of place on the table or over the mantle, give the counterbalance ball a little push, and the rowboat—already magically balanced—will rock backward and forward. This is a toy that will give a great deal of quiet contemplative pleasure to kids and adults alike.

One of the pleasures of making a toy such as this one is that you can chop and change the design to suit your own needs and fancies. For example, you might want to have two bears in the boat, or have a plane instead of a boat, or have the figures whittled rather than turned. Whatever you decide, the design is broad and flexible enough for you to change the details accordingly. Of course, if you like the idea of the toy, but don't have a lathe, there's no reason you can't whittle the bear to shape, use ready-made dowel for the two uprights, and have the base cut from a square slab.

Have a look at the working drawings on pages 117-119. The toy is made up from three primary parts: the turned stand with the doughnut ring base, the two pillar-like poles, and the crossbar. The bear is made up from six turnings: a head, a body, and four sausage-like arms. The boat is carved dish-like from a solid block of wood.

Study the details and note carefully how the toy is put together, with the poles being spigot-mortised into the base ring, the crossbar glued and pinned on top of the poles, the turned limbs and the head glue-fixed to the body, and all the little fixtures and fittings glued to the boat.

Consider how the success of the toy (the angle and stability of the "magical" balance) depends on the weight of the counterbalance bob and the length and shape of the counterbalance wire. Keep in mind that if you use heavier wood, you need a slightly longer boat, and so on, so you might have to modify the curve of the wire and the size of the bob to suit your particular toy.

Skill level I think it fair to say that this toy must be rated as one of the most difficult in the book—not so much because the individual techniques are in any way complicated, but rather because the design involves using several techniques (turning, carving, whittling, and scroll saw work). That said, if you have a lathe, a scroll saw, a selection of woodcarving tools—and if you are

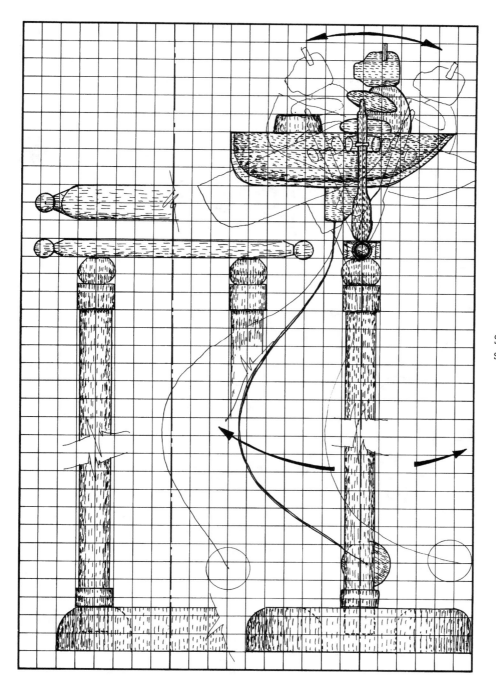

Scale: 2 grid
squares=1 inch

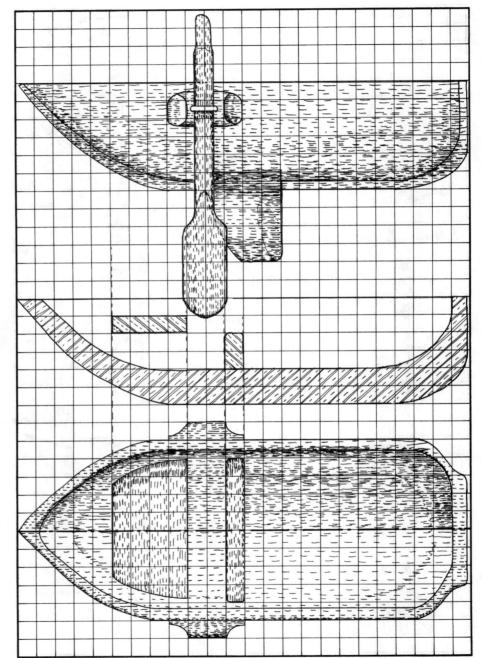

Scale: 4 grid
squares=1 inch

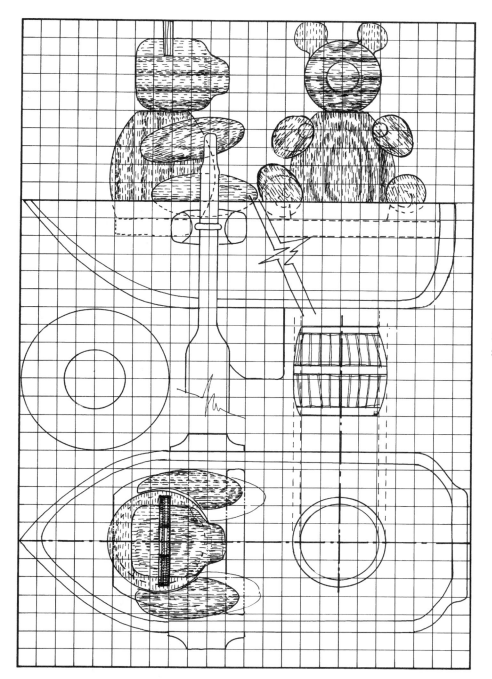

Scale: 4 grid
squares=1 inch

something more than a beginner—then this project is going to be a cinch.

Carving the rowboat

Draw the various component parts up to full size and take tracings. Then check that all your wood is in good condition, and set the 6-inch length of wood (the bit for the rowboat) flat-down on the workbench. Use a pencil, ruler, and square to establish an end-to-end centerline, and identify and pencil-label the faces "top," "side," and "front."

Take the traced profiles of the side and top views and pencil-press transfer the traced lines through to the appropriate faces of the wood, as shown. Now, starting with the side view, run the wood through the scroll saw and cut away the areas of primary waste.

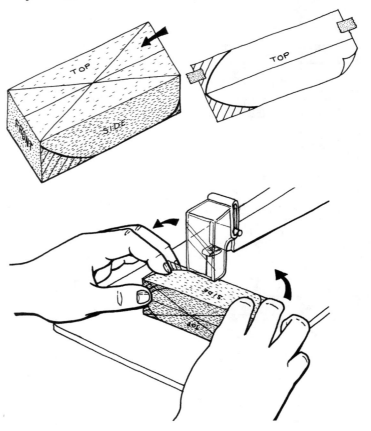

When you have achieved the basic boat shape, carefully draw in on the top view the area that needs to be scooped away and lowered. The top rim or lip of the boat should be about ¼ inch thick. It's a good idea to establish the depth by drilling a depth hole down into the center.

Now, working with the boat block secured top-side-up in the jaws of the vise, take the spoon bit gouge or a bent deep V gouge and set to work scooping out the inside shape of the boat. Work slowly around the rim, all the while cutting away shallow scoops of waste, and always cutting from side-to-center.

The procedure is beautifully easy. Simply lower the whole area of waste in stages or steps, skimming off one ⅛-inch-thick layer and then another, and so on, until you have scooped out the center of the boat to a depth of about 1 inch. It's easy enough, as long as you go at it slowly, remembering all the while to slope and curve the sides so as to make the inside-boat shape. Don't force the tool in too deep, and be sure to stop every now and again to recheck the depth of waste and the total thickness of the wood. When you reach the 1-inch-at-center depth, then rework the whole of the inside of the boat to a smooth, tool-scooped texture.

Set the hollowed-out hull bottom-side-up on the worksurface, and draw in the central keel strip and the shape of the transom, as shown. This done, settle yourself down in a chair, protect your lap with a stout apron, and set to work whittling the outside of the boat to a good finish. Hold the boat bottom-side-up in one hand, hold the knife in the other hand, and then,

Hull

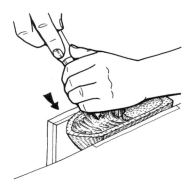

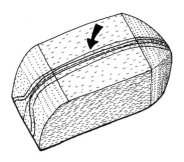

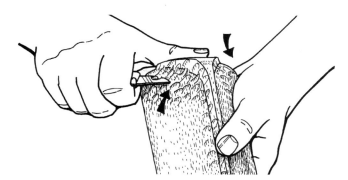

just as you might peel an apple, clear away the waste with small, tight, thumb-braced paring strokes.

Work one side of the boat and then the other, all the while working at an angle to the grain. If at any point along the way you have doubts as to how such-and-such a detail ought to go, best take a small piece of Plasticine and make a working model as a guide to size and form. When you have achieved what you think is a good boat shape, then take the scalpel or a fine-point penknife and work backward and forward over the boat, bringing all the small details to good order.

Fixtures   Look again at the working drawing on page 118 and see how the basic rowboat hull is fitted out with a number of additional fixtures—the seat, a footbrace, two rowlock blocks or mounts, and the keel block.

Seat   Starting with the seat, take a 1-inch-wide, ¼-inch-thick, 2-inch length of easy-to-carve wood, and use a knife to cut it to shape. Although the curved shape of the seat ends will relate to the shape of the inside of the hull, aim to have the seat about ¼ to ½ inch down from the rim and set about 1¼ inches along from the prow (the sharp end). It's quite difficult, so go at it little by little. Whittle the ends back a little bit, and then have a fitting. Cut back a little more and have another fitting, and so on, until the seat comes to a nice snug fit across the width of the boat.

Footbrace   Work the footbrace in more or less the same manner as the seat. The only difference is that you start with a smaller section of wood. Use the Super Glue to fix both the seat and the brace in position.

Rowlock blocks   When you come to the rowlock blocks, take a 2-inch-long piece of ½-x-¼-inch section wood (or a bit bigger; it doesn't really matter), and cut it into two 1-inch lengths. Next, having established that the ½-inch-wide face is "side," use the knife to scoop out the little end curves that make up the design. Aim to have the scooped ends about ¼ inch long and gently curving down from the ½-inch-square central section.

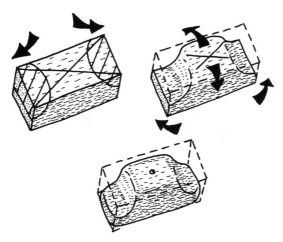

When you have swiftly whittled the two little lengths of wood to shape, round off the corners. Scoop away the backs so that they come to a good flush fit against the side of the hull, and fit in place with the Super Glue. Have the rowlock mounts set about ⅛ inch down from the top edge/rim and centered about 2½ inches along from the prow end.

Keel blocks

Look at the working drawing again on page 118 and see how the keel block is arranged with the grain running from front to back, so as to avoid having the wire set directly into end grain.

Whittle a 1¼-inch-square block of wood to shape. Carve and curve the top of the keel block so that it's a close mating fit to the underside of the hull. Glue-fix the block directly to the underside of the keel so that it is set about halfway along the 6-inch boat length.

Oars

Finally, take a couple of 4-inch-long, ½-x-¼-inch-section easy-to-carve offcuts and use the knife to whittle the two oars to shape, as shown. Aim for shafts at about ¼ inch diameter, round-ended blades at about ½ inch wide and ⅛ inch thick, and handles that taper from ¼ inch through to ³⁄₁₆ inch in diameter.

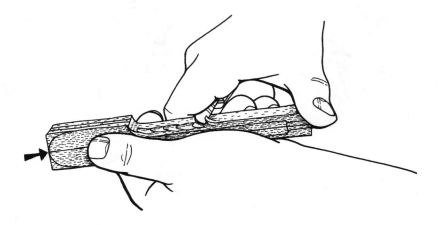

Turnings for the bear

Study the project picture and the working drawings on pages 113, 118, & 119 so that you have a clear picture in your mind of what goes where and how. Take your 14-inch length of 1¾-x-1¾-inch-section American southern yellow pine and establish the end centerpoints by setting the ends out with crossed diagonals.

This done, mount the four-jaw chuck on the lathe, and secure the wood in the chuck. Wind up the tailstock center and set the T-rest slightly below center of spin. Make sure that you and the lathe are in good safe order (see the lathe checklist in the glossary), and switch on the power.

Take the round-nosed gouge and make a few passes to clear away the corner waste, and then continue until the wood is a 1½-inch-diameter cylindrical section. Take the ruler and dividers and, working from left to right, mark the still-spinning wood with all the stepoffs that make up the design. See the illustration shown below.

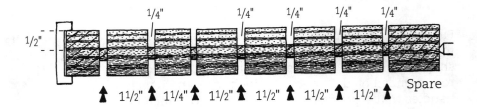

Allowing about 1½ inches for chuck waste, follow through with:

- 1½ inches for the body
- ¼ inch for waste
- 1¼ inches for the head
- ¼ inch for waste
- Four stepoffs of 1½ inches with ¼ inch of waste in between for each of the limbs

The remaining length of wood, between the last limb and the tailcenter, can be used for spare. It's a good idea when you are turning identical multiples like the limbs to turn off an extra one, and then to choose the best-matched four.

When you are happy with the way the wood is set out, take the ¼-inch-wide parting tool and sink all the waste areas in to a depth of ½ inch. Reckon on leaving a ½-inch-diameter central core.

Starting with the body and the head, take the skew chisel and set to work turning off the sharp corners and turning the head and the body to shape. Run the chisel with the grain from high to low wood—from the widest part of the body, and down and around into the waste, as shown. If you are a beginner and a bit wary about using a skew chisel, try using either a small, round-nosed gouge or a scraper.

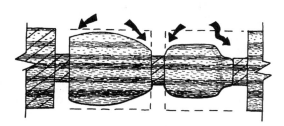

When you have achieved the body and the head, work along the limbs and turn them down to the ½-inch-diameter core size. Reestablish the limb stepoff lengths, cut the waste areas in deeper, and then repeat the rounding-off procedure and turn each limb to a nicely rounded sausage shape. Use the graded sandpaper to rub the turnings down to a smooth finish.

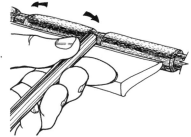

When you have achieved all the turnings, draw the tailstock center back out of the way, and use the skew chisel to carefully part off the individual shapes. The procedure is simple enough: Cut off the tailstock waste and bring the end of the first limb in line to a round-ended conclusion. Then part that limb off from its neighbor, while at the same time turning the other end to a good finish, and so on along the line of turnings. Go at it slowly and carefully, cupping the work in one hand, while at the same time nipping it off with the skew chisel.

While the lathe is at hand, and working in the way as already described, check with the working drawings another time. Then take a length of 2-inch-square-section scrap and turn off the little barrel shape and the counterbalance ball.

Assembly

Take the six turnings that make the bear—the body, the head, and the four limbs—and give them a final rubdown with a fine-grade sandpaper to take the parting-off area to a good, smooth finish. Next, set the head on the body, note any rough or proud areas that need to be cut back, and then use a knife or sandpaper to work the wood accordingly. It's best to slice off one side of the head and the top of the body, so that the two mating faces come together for a flat fit.

Establish the position of the ears, and take a small tenon or gents saw and cut a ¼-inch-deep, ⅛-inch-wide slot along the line of the ears, across the width of the head. Then cut the two-ear shape from a scrap of ⅛-inch ply and glue-fix it in place in the slot (see project 12).

Set the bear on the rowboat seat. Decide where the arms and legs need to be set in relationship to the sides of the boat and the foot brace, and mark the side of the limbs and the body accordingly. This done, take a knife and slice back mating faces so that they all come together for a smooth, tight, flush fit.

Finally, when you have sliced back waste areas and generally decided what goes where and how, dribble Super Glue on mating faces and fit the six component parts together—the head to the top, and the arms and legs to the side of the body.

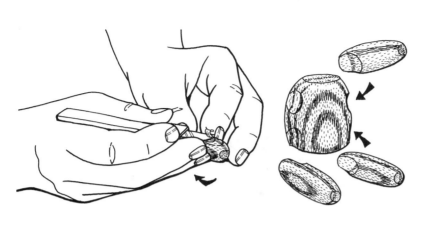

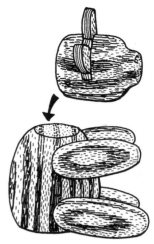

Making the stand

Take the 6½-x-6½-inch slab (the piece for the base), and establish its center by drawing crossed diagonals. Fix the compass to a radius of 3 inches, and set the face of the slab out with a 6-inch-diameter circle. Use the scroll saw to cut out the circle and to clear away the waste.

Cut a 6-inch-diameter circle from a sheet of carton cardboard. Now, having made sure that the screws occur about 1 inch in from the side of the circle (well clear of the central area that's going to be cut away), set the cardboard waster between the faceplate and the workpiece. Run screws through the faceplate and into the wood, as shown. When you are happy that all is correct, mount the faceplate on the lathe. Push the tailstock well back out of the way, bring the tool rest up to the wood so that you can work it face-on, and then switch on the power.

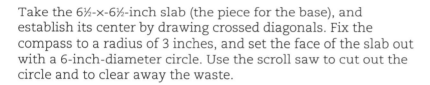

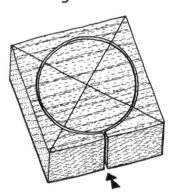

First take the parting tool or the skew chisel and run it straight into the spinning disc to clear away the waste and turn it down to a smooth-edged 6-inch diameter. Next, take the round-nosed gouge and skim back the face of the disc until it's smooth and even. With the dividers fixed to a radius of 1 inch, set the point

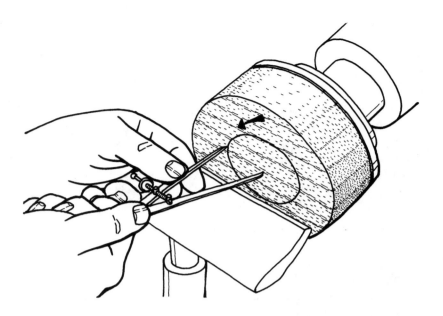

on center-of-spin, support the dividers on the tool rest and scribe the disc out with a 2-inch-diameter inner circle.

Take the tool of your choice (you may use a parting tool, a gouge, or a skew chisel), and remove the central 2-inch circle so that you are left with a 6-inch-diameter, 2-inch-wide hoop or *quoit*. Use the skew chisel to cut back the sharp corners/edges, and turn the wood down to a smooth-shouldered ring.

Having used the sandpaper to rub the wood down to a smooth finish, use the point of the skew chisel to cut a V-groove guide for the poles, 1 inch in from the outside of the ring. Then remove the faceplate from the lathe and the wood from the faceplate. Finally, mark in the position of the two poles and use a ½-inch-diameter bit to sink ¾-inch-deep blind holes for the pole spigots.

Turning the poles

Take the 30-inch length of 1¼-x-1¼-inch-section wood, and check it over to make sure that it is completely clear of splits and knots. Find the end-center points by drawing crossed diagonals, and mount the wood securely on the lathe, between the chuck and the tailstock center.

First turn the square section wood down to a cylindrical section, and then turn the cylinder down to a smooth, 1-inch diameter. Fix the dividers to a radius of ¾ inch and step-off the measurement that make up the decorative features at each end of the pillars. Working from left to right along the wood, and following the illustration shown, allow:

- 1½ inches for chuck waste
- ¾ inch for the first pole spigot
- ¾ inch for the foot of the pillar
- 11 inches for the shaft
- ¾ inch for the capital
- ¾ inch for the ball
- ¼ inch for waste
- Then reverse the measurements for the other pillar.

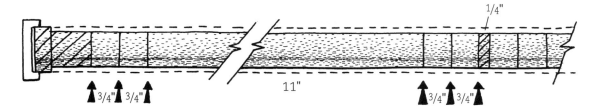

Note that the pillars are set head-to-head so that you can compare the shapes and make a good match.

Having established all the stepoffs, take the skew chisel and lower the main shaft (the straight area between the foot and the capital) by about ⅛ inch. Reduce the spigot areas in like manner. Aim for shafts at about ¾ inch in diameter. When you have achieved the shafts, take the skew chisel and turn the

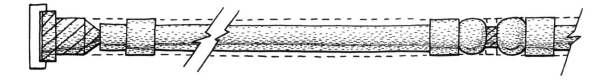

top-of-pillar areas down to balls. Don't worry too much about trying to achieve perfect spheres; ours are, in fact, slightly flattened. Just try for two shapes that are nicely matched. Take these to a good, smooth finish and part off.

Turning the cross-beam

Take the 12-inch length of 1-x-½-inch-section wood (the piece for the cross-beam) and find the end-center points by drawing crossed diagonals. Use a knife or chisel to shave the chuck end of the wood down to a square section, as shown.

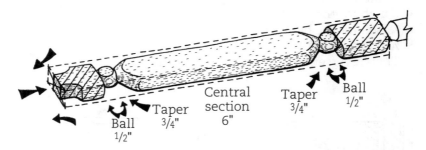

Ball 1/2"   Taper 3/4"   Central section 6"   Taper 3/4"   Ball 1/2"

Mount the wood between lathe center, and check that you and the lathe are in good safe order. Bring the tool rest up so that it is a little below spin height, and switch on the power. Take the dividers and, working from left to right along the wood, set out all the stepoffs that make up the design. Allow:

- 1½ inches for headstock waste
- ½ inch for the end bead/ball
- ¾ inch for the taper
- 6 inches for the straight central section
- ¾ inch for the other taper
- ½ inch for the other bead/ball
- the rest for tailstock waste

Take the round-nosed gouge and very carefully make a couple of passes along the work, just enough to trim back the sharp corners. Now, turn the bead/ball stepoff down to a ½-inch-diameter cylinder, and run the taper from the ½-x-1-inch section through to what will be the start of the ball.

Turn the balls to a round finish. Rub the whole workpiece down to a smooth finish, and part off. If all is well, the rectangular 1-x-½-inch section should run in a smooth taper from the central section through to the balls, as shown in the illustration.

Super-Glue the pillar spigots in the base holes, and glue and pin the cross-beam across the top of the pillars. Make sure that the whole structure is fair and square, and put it to one side until the glue is dry.

Assembly of stand

Having made the bear, the boat, and the stand, wipe away all the dust and move to the dust-free area that you have set aside for painting. Study the painting grid shown on page 132. Start by painting the inside of the boat and the counterbalance weight light blue, and the outside of the boat white. Next, paint the bear's little vest bright red.

Painting & finishing

When the areas of ground color are completely dry, use the fine-point brush to paint in all the details: the blue-and-red stripe around the outside of the hull, the red transom, keel strip, oar handles and rowlock mounts, and all the other little details that make up the design. Of course, if you want to go for different colors, or give the boat a name, then now's the time to do it.

When the paint is dry, clench the screw-eyes around the oars and screw-fix them in place on the rowlock mounts. Next, glue-fix the bear and the barrel in place in the rowboat. Bend the length of coat hanger wire more or less into the shape illustrated, and drill-spike and glue it into the keel block on the underside of the boat, and into the counterbalance ball. Sit the boat in place on top of the stand and adjust the wire until the boat is nicely balanced.

Finally, give the whole toy—the boat, the bear, and the stand—a couple of coats of clear varnish, and Barnacle Boatman Bear is ready for his first row, row, row.

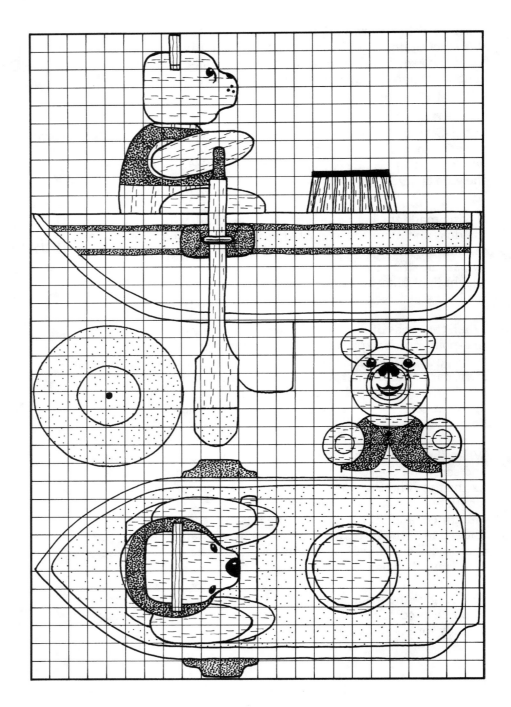

- We use Super Glue because it is so swift and non-messy, the job is done and finished in a few minutes.
- Not to worry if you don't have a four-jaw chuck. You could modify the stages and settle for turning between centers.
- If you don't want to go to the trouble of turning a barrel and a counterbalance ball, then you could use found objects like kids' play bricks, or even large wooden beads or skittle balls.
- If you only have a short-bed lathe, and so have to turn the pillars separately, remember to allow for twice as much end waste.
- Having said that you need coat-hanger wire (meaning galvanized wire at about $\frac{1}{8}$ to $\frac{3}{16}$ inch in diameter), you could use just about any wire that will bend easily and hold its shape.
- We favor using jelutong because it is easy to turn, easy to carve, a good light color, and—perhaps most important of all—it is a swift-growing, sustainable wood.
- You could modify the design and carve a counterbalance weight in the shape of a large fish, or an anchor, or a mermaid.
- When you have painted the black face details on the bear, use the fine-point brush and white paint to spot on the highlights of the nose and eyes.

Roly-Poly,
the teddy rattle

R OLY-POLY, the teddy bear rattle, was one of those friendly, happy little girl bears who just liked nothing better than to shake up and down and make music. Her favorite dances were the rumba, the samba, and conga.

> I like to shimmy
> I like to shake
> Just you listen
> To the music I make!
>
> Roly-Poly rumba
> Rotating to the song
> Let's all do the conga
> Let's all dance along

Roly-Poly is a turned rattle or shaker—a nice comfort toy for a baby or toddler. This project involves using the lathe, drill, and spoon gouge on American southern yellow pine, and it practices the techniques of chuck turning, hollow turning, drilling, and working with a carver's gouge.

Materials

14" length of strong-grained, easy-to-turn wood at 2½" square (We used American southern yellow pine)
Workout & tracing paper
Handful of dried lentils or peas for the noisemakers
Cardboard for templates
Short length of cord (about 8")
Super Glue
Small amount of black matte acrylic paint
Clear, high-shine varnish

Tools

Woodturning lathe with a four-jaw chuck to fit
Good selection of woodturning tools, (include a round-nosed gouge, a parting tool, & a skew chisel)
Compass
Dividers
Calipers
Drill chuck to fit the tailstock end of the lathe, with a ¾" bit to fit
Pillar/bench drill with bits at ⅛" & ½"

Small spoonbit woodcarving gouge
Pencil
Ruler
Soft-haired paintbrushes, medium & fine

Looking &
planning

Roly-Poly, the teddy rattle is a beautiful toy, beloved by children and adults alike. For kiddies of a certain age, she is the perfect comforter and companion. She is good to hold, she is beautiful to look at, and, perhaps best of all, she makes a very satisfying *shssss shssss* sound.

Have a look at the working drawings on pages 138 and 139, and note how important it is, in the context of toys that are going to be cuddled and sucked, that the total form be smoothly contoured and altogether kiddy-friendly. There should be no thin sections or sharp corners.

From the woodworker's viewpoint, the project is exciting in that it is a not-so-easy multi-technique challenge. The actual form of the toy is relatively uncomplicated and straightforward. There are no hinged or pivotal parts. Nevertheless, because there needs to be a good head-to-body fit and because the body has to be hollowed out, the order of work and the various stages require some extra consideration. Be mindful, before you start the project, that the turning is relatively tricky. Also, the drilling calls for a fair amount of careful measuring and placing, and the hollow turning and gouge carving does require a deal of skill and care.

Study the way the project is turned all of one piece. The bear handle and body, the head, the two ears, and the nose are all turned from the same length of wood. The primary outside forms are turned first, then the neck spigot is cut and the head removed, the body drilled, and so on. Finally, note how the turned profiles are checked using cardboard template profiles.

Skill level

This is one of those projects that can only be successfully managed if you have the right tools and equipment. You need a good, solid woodturning lathe with a special chuck. We use a heavy-duty four-jaw chuck. You also need a tailstock drill

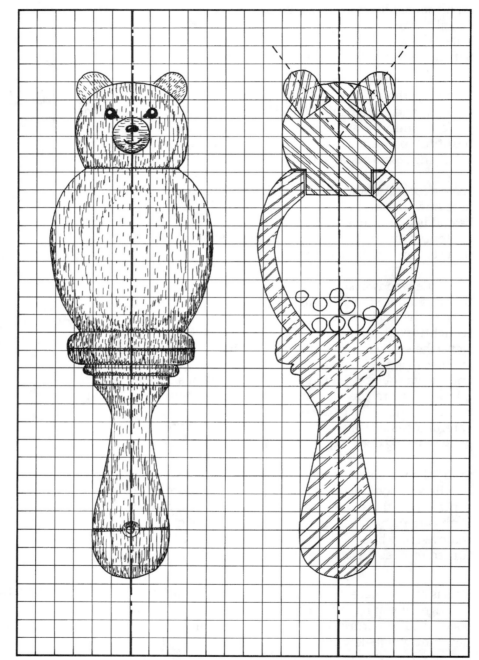

Scale: 4 grid
squares=1 inch

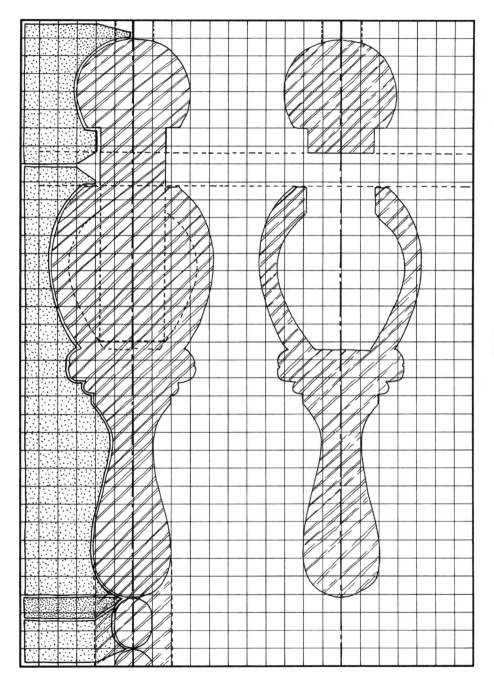

Scale: 4 grid
squares=1 inch

Roly-Poly, the teddy rattle   139

chuck. That said, if you have a liking for making small, precisely turned, beautifully finished items, then this is the project for you.

Mounting the wood

Draw your designs up to size and make sure that you have established good, clean, workable profiles. Make careful tracings, and pencil-press transfer the various profiles through to your pieces of template card. Next, line in the three template sections (the head and neck spigot, the bear-body-handle, and one of the three identical beads) and cut them out.

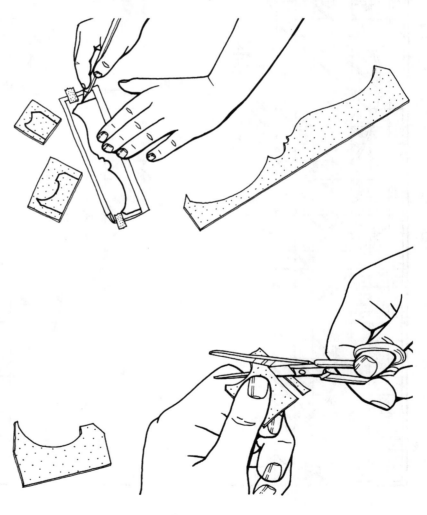

Now take the 14-inch length of southern yellow pine and check it over just to make sure that it is free from splits, dead knots, and stains. Draw diagonals across the square-cut ends of the wood and establish the end centerpoints. Punch in the centerpoint on the tailstock end of the wood, position the other end in the four-jaw chuck, and then secure the work by clamping the tailstock in position and running the dead-center tightly into the wood. When the chuck has been tightened and the wood is secure, ease back the tailstock center just a fraction, and oil the spin hole. Finally, position the tool rest so that it is as close as possible to the work and a little below the centerline.

When you have run through your pre-switch-on checklist (see glossary), switch on the power. Take the round-nosed chisel and start by making a few practice runs up and down the work, just to get the feel of your tool and the wood. For the first few cuts the tool will bump and judder, so hold the tool firmly and progress slowly until you have turned off the unevenness.

Roughing out

When you have achieved a good 2¼" cylinder, use the pencil, ruler and dividers to set the wood out with all the stepoffs that go to make up the design. Starting at the headstock, and allowing no more than 2 inches for chuck waste, set out:

- 2 inches for the ear and nose beads
- 2¾ inches for the handle
- ¼ inch for the small decorative bead at the top of the handle
- ½ inch for the generous bead under the bear's body
- 2¼ inches for the body
- ¾ inch for waste and the head spigot
- 1¼ inches for the head itself
- The rest for tailstock waste

Follow the illustration from left to right as you make the stepoffs.

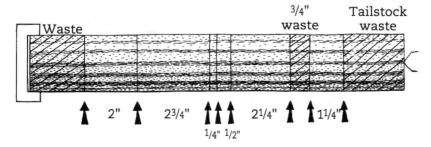

Turning the head

When you are happy with the way the wood has been set out, have another look at the details just to make sure that you are clear in your own mind as to how the various stages need to be worked. Now, take the parting tool, and sink the ¾-inch-long neck-spigot area until you are left with a central core cylinder that is about ⅞ inch in diameter.

This done, set the calipers to 1½ inches, and then use the tool of your choice to turn the head down to 1½ inches diameter. Next take the skew chisel and very carefully turn the head down to shape. Work at it slowly, making plenty of stop-offs along the way to check the turning off against the cardboard template.

When you have achieved what you consider is a good head shape, then rub it down with the fine-grade sandpaper until it is super-smooth. Make sure that the workpiece is well-secured in the four-jaw chuck, and leave about ⅜ inch for the neck spigot. Then cut away the bulk of waste from between the top of the head and the tailstock, and from between the spigot and the body. Support the head in one hand, and very carefully part the head off from the cone of tailstock waste and the workpiece.

Turning the body

Having parted off the head, draw the tailstock back out of the way, switch the lathe at a slower speed, and use the point of the skew chisel to carefully establish a center-point "dimple" on the solid neck end of the body. Reposition the tailstock and wind the center in so that the workpiece is once again supported at both ends, and turn up the speed.

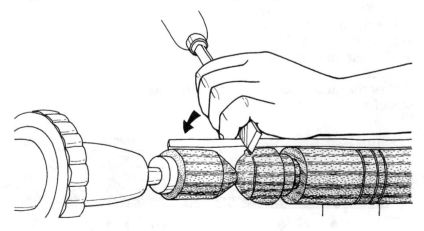

Now take the parting and the skew chisel and, using the templates as a guide, work along the cylinder cutting in all the curves, dips, and beads that make up the design. One step at a time, cut the barrel-shaped body, the step-and-bead at the top of the handle, and the curves that go to make the handle. NOTE: At this stage, don't attempt to finalize the end of the handle or the beads. Continue working back and forth along the workpiece until you have what you consider is a nicely turned form. When you are happy with the turning, use the fine-grade sandpaper to rub the work down to a smooth finish.

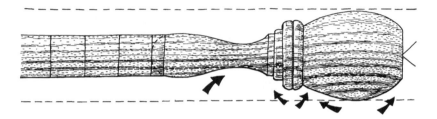

Draw the tailstock back and fit the tailstock drill chuck with your ¾-inch drill bit. Now, with great caution, switch on the lathe and carefully run the drill bit into the body of the bear to a depth of about 2¼ inches. Don't try to sink the hole in one great thrust. It's much better to wind the drill in a little, withdraw it to remove some of the waste, wind it in a little more, and so on. Gradually work deeper and deeper into the wood until the hole is the correct depth.

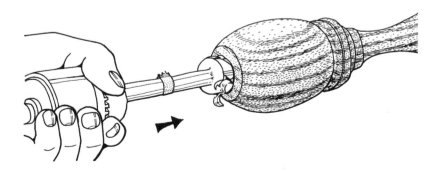

The hole finished, set the tool rest up near the end of the handle and use the skew chisel to finalize the end of the handle and to part the body-handle off from the remaining 2 inches of wood. Finally, turn the three identical bead/bullet shapes that make up the two ears and the nose.

Carving out the body

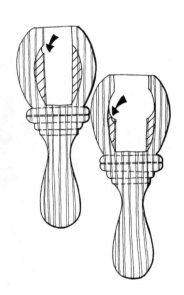

When you have achieved the five elements that make up the bear shaker—the body-handle, the head-stopper, the nose, and the two ears—move away from the lathe and settle down in a comfortable sitting position. Now hold the handle-bear in one hand, just as you might hold a boiled egg in an egg-cup. Take the spoon bit gouge in the other hand, and set to work making the ¾-inch-wide sinking deeper and wider. Again, don't try to remove the waste in a single, great thrust; it's much better to scoop out the waste little by little, turning and scooping as you go.

Continue turning and scooping, turning and scooping, until the cylindrical sinking widens and the walls are reduced in thickness. It's all pretty straightforward, as long as the gouge is sharp, and as long as you don't dig the gouge too deep and try to remove too much waste in a single cut. The only thing that you do have to watch out for is that you don't lever the metal shank of the tool against the rim of the bear's neck. Try to achieve a smooth interior so that the lentils can roll around freely.

Assembly & painting

When you have taken the hollowing out as far as you want it to go, then comes the very satisfying tasks of putting the bear together and painting it.

Start by making sure that the head spigot is a good fit. If need be, reduce the diameter of the spigot with a knife and/or sandpaper. Next mark off the position of the cord hole at a point about ½ to ¾ inch along from the end of the handle, and run the hole through with the ⅛-inch-diameter drill bit.

When you come to fitting the two ears (the two bead shapes), start by drawing in on the head an over-the-head centerline. Make sure that the line runs squarely with the direction of the grain. Fix the compass to a radius of about ½ inch, spike the point at top-center, and draw a circle on top of the head. The ears can be set at the two circle centerline crossover points. Establish the position of the nose so that it relates to the two ears.

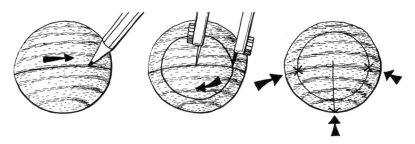

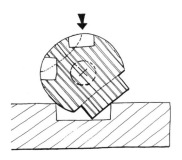

Set the ½ inch diameter bit in the pillar/bench/press drill and support the head on a predrilled block of waste wood. Run the ear and nose holes in to depth of about ½ inch. Try to angle the drill so that all three holes run squarely into the wood, and so that the two ears are symmetrical.

Having drilled out the three holes, trim the three beads to a good, tight push-fit and glue them in position. Now pop the lentils or peas in the body cavity and glue the head-stopper in place. Make sure that the head is aligned and set so that there is a nice match-up between the head and body grain.

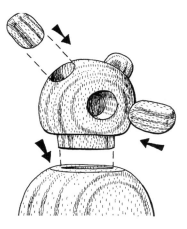

Give the whole workpiece a fine sanding to remove rough grain and glue ooze, and thread a short length of cord through the handle hole. Tie the cord to make a hanging.

Let the paint and varnish dry between coats. Then give the whole workpiece a thin coat of varnish, and paint in the face details with the fine-point brush and the black acrylic paint. Give the bear a couple more coats of varnish, and Roly-Poly is ready to shake.

Roly-Poly, the teddy rattle **145**

Special tips

- Be warned! You can only make this project in the way described if you are using a really good chuck system—one that is sure to hold the workpiece secure. If you have any doubts as to whether your chosen system is safe and secure, then ask a more experienced woodturner for guidance.
- Bearing in mind that woodturning is, by its very nature, potentially dangerous, try to make a habit of running through your pre-switch-on checklist before switching on the power (see glossary).
- Using the spoon gouge is easy, but only if the blade is sharp and you settle for removing thin curls of wood. If you have any doubts as to how best to hold and manage the gouge, then have a pre-project tryout on some scrap wood.
- When you are using the gouge, hold it low, down near the blade, and remove the waste wood with a small, tight, controlled scoop-and-dig action, much as you might scoop out a boiled egg.
- If you have a power-tool carver/sander, then you could use it to remove the inside-body waste.

Teddy truckers

BIG BOSS, the teddy bear trucker, was just about the happiest teddy in the whole wide world. The sun was shining, there was a heap of food packed away in the truck—lots of cakes, jelly, ice cream, chocolate, and soda pop—his teddy trucker friends were around, and they were all going on a picnic . . . yummy! "Who wants what?" shouted Alan Big Boss bear.

"I want the chocolate," squeaked Busybody Bear.

"I want jelly," growled Brawny Bear.

"I want cake," bellowed Burley Bear.

"I want ice cream," laughed Buxom Bear.

"I want pop, " whispered Bashful Bear.

> Six teddy truckers,
> Going for a ride,
> All the teddies on the back,
> All the food inside!
>
> Six little teddy bears,
> Yum-yum yummy.
> Where's all the food gone?
> Down in the tummy!

The teddy truckers toy is a push-along truck with Crosley 1940 imagery and six peg-fit teddy bears. The project requires the use of a lathe, a scroll saw, a flat saw, and a drill, as well as multicore plywood, jelutong, American southern yellow pine, and plastic wheels. Making the project, you will practice the techniques of turning, fretting, drilling, shaping, and painting.

Materials   Best-quality ½"-thick multicore plywood, 13" × 5½" wide for the chassis
Jelutong
   3" × 3" square, 4" long for the truck cab
   1½" × 3", 8" long for the hood/front of the truck
   5" × 1½", 5" long, for the base of the truck

Offcuts for the headlamps & front-wheel arches

10" length of prepared wood, ½"×¾" section, for the two over-back-wheel strips

1¼" wide slice from end of a ¾"-thick, 6"-wide plank for the two wheel-axle blocks

30" length of 1½"× 1½" square section American southern yellow pine for the six teddy bears

Best-quality ⅛"-thick multicore plywood, small quantity, for the six sets of ears

Four 2"-diameter plastic truck wheels

Four 1½"-long round-end chrome screws to fit the wheels

Screws for the fittings & trim

Two bottles Super Glue

Workout & tracing paper

Acrylic paints in red, green, & black for the truck; yellow & two shades of blue for the bear's stripes

Graded sandpapers

Clear, high-shine varnish

Woodturning lathe with a four-jaw chuck

Small gents saw

Workbench & vise

Electric scroll saw with heavy-duty blade & 3" cutting height

Bench drill with bits at ¾" & ¼"

Screwdriver to fit the screws

Pencil

Ruler

Try square

Compass

Marking gauge

Good selection of turning tools

Dividers

Calipers

Small block plane

Open-toothed Surform rasp

Soft-haired paintbrushes, broad & fine

Looking & planning

The 1940 Crosley truck, complete with six peg teddy bears, red and black plastic easy-turn wheels, and lots of trim and details, is a delightful push-around-the-carpet toy. If you enjoy a whole range of woodworking activities—woodturning, using the scroll saw, and general shaping and construction—and if you know of a child who likes automobiles, then I've got a feeling that this is going to be the project for you.

Look at the working drawings on pages 151 and 152, to see how the truck is put together. The chassis is cut from a ½-inch-thick sheet of best-quality multicore plywood, and the cab, hood, and various bits and pieces are fitted as separate glue-fixed additions. See how we have used four good-quality, plastic truck wheels. Note also how the bed at the back of the truck is kept clear of the back wheels by being mounted up on two thin, across-chassis sections.

Finally, when you have studied the working drawings, noted all the tool and material implications of working a project of this size, and generally considered possible design modifications, then draw the design up to full size and make tracings.

Skill level

Although each of the individual stages is relatively simple and direct, you do, of course, need to have a lathe and a scroll saw, and you need to be experienced in a broad range of woodworking activities. That said, if you like the idea of the truck, but don't have the lathe and the saw, then you can modify the design, and, for example, have the teddies made from whittled broomstick dowel and the various large blocks fretted out with a coping saw. You might have to change some of the details, and the project will certainly take longer to complete, but you should be able to get the truck made.

Cutting the chassis base

Decide what wood you are going to use, and generally gather together all your tools and materials. Then start by setting out the chassis base. Check over the sheet of ½-inch-thick plywood to make sure that it's in good order. Then with pencil, measure, and square, set it out at about 4½ inches wide, 12 inches long. Make stepoffs from front to back on both side edges: ½ inch, 1 inch, 2¼ inches for the front wheels, 4 inches for the running board, 2¼ inches for the back wheels, 1½ inches and ½ inch.

When you are happy with the setting out, run little pencil curves around all angles so that all the corners are smooth and

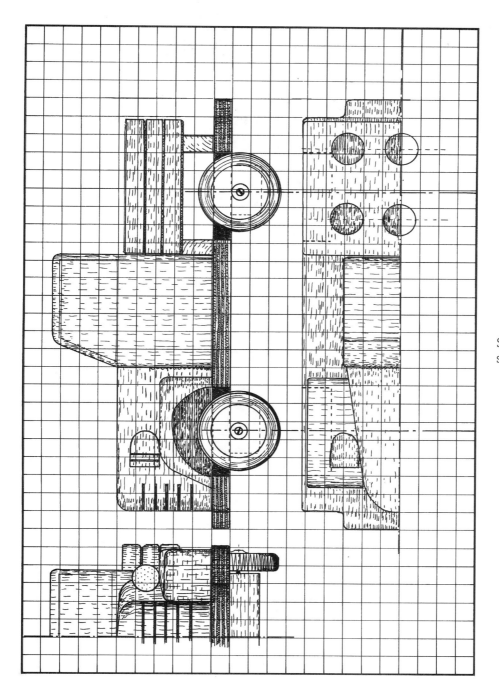

Teddy truckers   151

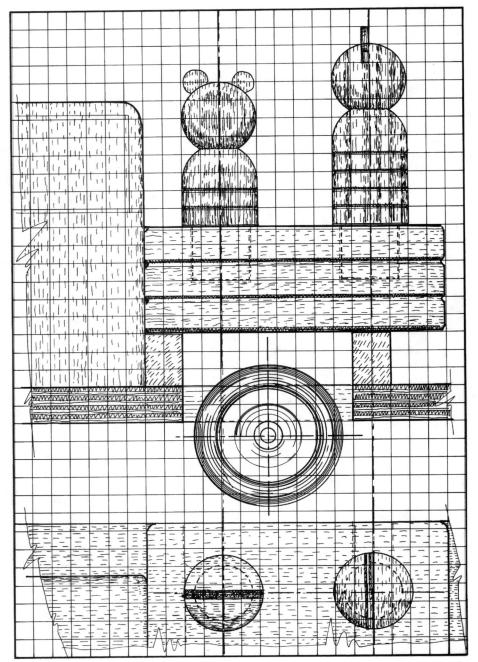

Scale: 4 grid
squares=1 inch

user-friendly. Take the plywood to the scroll saw and set to work fretting out the form.

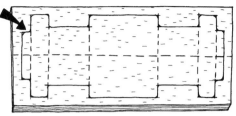

It's all pretty straightforward: Just run and feed the wood into the blade so that the line of cut is a little to the waste side of the drawn line. Don't push the workpiece so fast that the blade tears up the grain or go so slow that the blade marks time and friction burns the wood. If you are a raw beginner, it might be a good idea to have a tryout with some scrap wood.

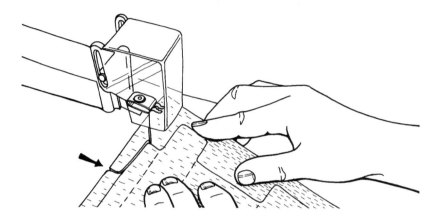

Take the 4-inch length of 3-x-3-inch-square section wood and check it over to make sure that it is free from difficult-to-work flaws like hard knots and splits. Now, having marked the faces "top," "front," "side," and "back," measure 2½ inches up from bottom on the front, and 2½ inches along from back to front on the top.

Draw straight lines to define the shape of the cab, set the block of wood side-down on the scroll saw table, and slice away the triangle of waste. (If don't have a scroll saw, use a flat hand saw.)

Next, take the graded sandpapers and rub the cab shape down so that all faces are smooth and all the top and side edges, angles, and corners are nicely curved and rounded. Make sure

Making the cab

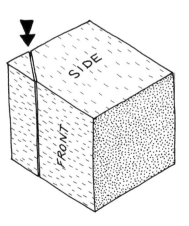

that the bottom is a good, smooth, square-edged fit so that the cab sits flat-down on the chassis.

Cutting the engine hood

Take the 8-inch length of 3-x-1½-inch section wood, and cut it down so that you have two pieces, each 4 inches long. Set the pieces side-by-side and mark in the various sides. Next, draw out the shape of the hood (see the plan on page 151). Make a tracing, and then pencil-press transfer the shape through to the top face of both pieces. When you are sure that all is correct, run the wood one block at a time through the scroll saw so as to cut out the round-fronted hood shape. Once again, if you don't have a scroll saw, then you will need to use a flat saw and a rasp.

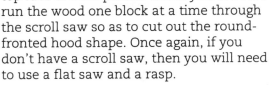

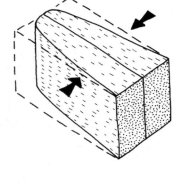

When you have achieved the hood shape, bond the two blocks of wood together. (We used Super Glue). Then use the plane and the rasp to shape all the smooth angles and corners.

With the hood secure front-end-up in the jaws of a rag-muffled vise, take the handsaw and run five cuts ½ inch down into the hood so as to create the radiator grill effect. Finally, just as with the cab, rub the base down so that the hood sits flat and square on the chassis.

Making the mudguards

Study the working drawings again, to see how the mudguards are shaped, placed, and fitted. Take a 3-inch length of 1½-x-3-inch easy-to-work wood, and set it flat down on the worksurface so that the 3-x-3-inch face is uppermost and so the end-grain face is facing front. Pencil-label the 3-x-1½-inch end-grain faces "front" and "back," and label the uppermost face "top." Take a pencil and ruler, and run a centerline from end to end, so that the top face is divided in half and so that the line starts and finishes on end grain.

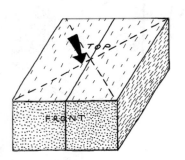

Next, flip the wood over so that one of the side faces is uppermost. Trace and pencil-press transfer the bridge shape through to the wood. Shade in the areas of waste. This done, run the block of wood slowly through the scroll saw and carefully cut away the waste.

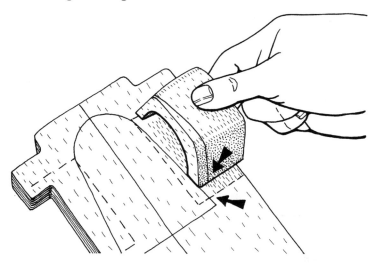

You should now have a long bridge shape at 3 inches wide, 3 inches long, and 1½ inches high. If all is correct and as described, set the bridge top-face-up, and run it through the scroll saw, slicing it in half along the centerline, so that you have two identical 1½-inch-wide mudguards.

Next—and this isn't easy—take the chassis base, and draw in the position of the hood and mudguards. Align the mudguard shapes at either side of the engine hood area, and very carefully draw in the angle lines that establish the mating fit of mudguard to hood. You should now have two identical but mirror-imaged mudguards.

When you are happy that all is correct, run the bridge shapes a piece at a time through the scroll saw, and cut away the waste. Finally, have a last fitting against the hood and the base, and sand and round off the top edges.

Making the truck bed

Take the 5-inch length of 5-inch-wide, 1½-inch-thick wood (you could have it closer to the finished size), and use the pencil, ruler, and square to set it out so that it is 4 inches long and 4½ inches wide. Use one of your saws to clear away the waste.

Next, set the wood down on the bench so that the 4-x-4½-inch face is uppermost, and pencil-label the 4½-inch-wide end-grain faces "front" and "back" and the uppermost face "top." Set out the six-hole grid for the six teddies (as shown on pages 151 and 152). The finished bears should be about 1 inch in diameter, the spigot/peg location holes should be ¾ inch wide, and the hole centers should be about 2 inches apart.

We have the bears set three at the front and three at the back, but there's no reason why you can't change the pattern and have an informal arrangement. Just make sure that there is at least ½ inch between neighboring bears and ½ inch between the bears and the edge of the 4-x-4½-inch bed.

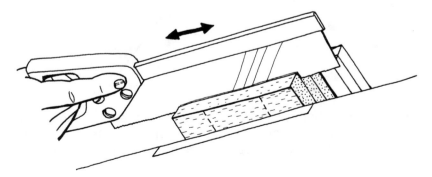

Set the marking gauge at ½ inch, and run it around both the bottom and top of the slab thickness to set out the three-plank pattern. When you are happy with the layout, take a tenon saw and cut each between-plank line in to a depth of about ⅛ to ¼ inch.

Next, having established the position of each of the six-hole centers, set the ¾-inch-diameter bit in the drill and run each hole down into the wood to a depth of about ¾ inch. Make sure that the holes are sunk so that they are true and at right angles to the top face of the wood.

Finally, take the graded sandpapers and rub all edges and faces down to a smooth finish. Aim for corners and edges that are slightly rounded.

Turning the teddies

Look over all the instructions in this project, and spend some time considering the tool, material, and technique implications of the toy. Ask yourself: Is my lathe big enough? Am I going to modify the scale and make the figures larger or smaller? Am I going to make all six figures identical?

When you have a clear image in your mind's eye of just how you want the teddies to be, sit down with the pencil, ruler, workout paper, and tracing paper, and draw the various figures out to full size.

Look at the drawings on pages 151 and 163. The scale is 4 grid squares to 1 inch, and all the bears are more or less the same size: The bodies are 1 inch in diameter, the heads are based on a 1-inch-diameter ball, the shoulders are a 1-inch-diameter half-ball, and the base peg spigots are ¾ inch in diameter and ¾ inch long. The teddies only appear to be variously taller and shorter because the bodies have been turned off at different lengths and the bands of color are varied.

When you are happy with your drawn images, pin them up out of harm's way, but within reach. Clear the workshop, and get ready for action. Make sure the American southern yellow pine is completely free from such nasties as dead knots, splits, and stains. Then take the 1½-x-1½-inch-square wood, and carefully establish the end centerpoints by drawing crossed diagonals.

With your dividers set to a radius of ½ inch, spike the dividers on the centerpoints, and scribe the ends of the wood out with circles. Do this at both ends. Draw tangents through the circle-diagonal intersections to set the ends of the wood out with octagons, and then establish the areas of waste by drawing octagon-linking lines from end-to-end along the length of the wood (see glossary).

Set the wood lengthwise in the vise so that one or other of the corners is uppermost, and use the plane to swiftly clear the bulk of the waste. Do this with all the corners. Don't fuss around; just reduce the waste so that the wood is more or less octagonal in section. NOTE: If you are using a good-size lathe you can skip this stage and turn the wood straight down from a square section.

Make sure that you and the lathe are in a good, safe working order. Check the on/off switch, set out the tools so that they are comfortably at hand, and generally make sure that all your flapping and trailing bits and pieces are either removed or at least tied back out of harm's way (see glossary).

When you are sure that everything is in good order, set the workpiece securely in the four-jaw chuck, wind up the tailstock center, and bring the tool rest up to the wood so that it is just a little below the center of spin. Turn the lathe over by hand to make sure that the wood clears the tool rest, and switch on the power.

Take the tool of your choice—we used a large, round-ended gouge—and make several swift passes from end to end along the wood until you achieve a smooth, 1-inch-diameter section. Keep the tool well braced with the handle down.

Having decided on how you want the six bears to be, use the dividers to transfer stepoff readings direct from the working drawings through to the spinning wood. Allowing at least ¼ inch of waste between figures, and work from left to right along the wood. Set out the following:

- about 1 inch for chuck waste
- ¾ inch for the first peg/spigot

- 1½ inch for the first body
- 1 inch for the first head
- ¼ inch of between-bear waste
- and so on with the other five bears

The only measurements that you need vary are the body lengths.

Note that the 30-inch length of wood allows you to make more bears than you need and then to select the best six.

When you are happy with the size and sequence of the stepoffs, then, one stepoff at a time and with the caliper set to ¾ inch, take the parting tool and reduce the neighboring bands of waste and spigot down to ¾ inch diameter. Having turned the 1-inch-diameter cylinder down to a series of steps, take the skew chisel and cut away the wood at the shoulders, neck, and the top of the head to create the fully rounded forms.

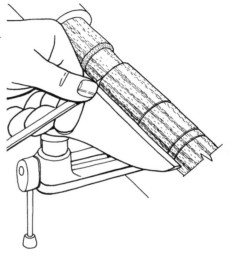

Working in the direction of the grain (from high down to low wood), slide the skew chisel over and down from the body into the neck, and from the head down to the neck, all the while removing the waste and getting closer and closer to the desired forms, as shown, left. When you have achieved a string or sequence of bears all set head-to-tail with each other, take the skew chisel and decorate each bear with V-section body grooves as shown, right.

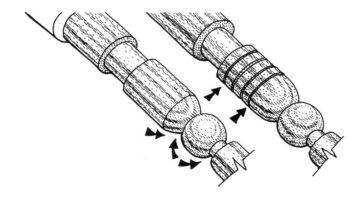

Next, starting at the tailstock end, reduce the waste as far as you dare, and then part off. Working from right to left along the wood the order of work should run:

1. Reduce the waste from between the bear head and the tailstock, and from between the bear's spigot and the next bear.
2. Use the fine-grade sandpaper to rub the turning down to a smooth finish.
3. Part off the bear.
4. Wind the tailstock up to support the next bear along
5. . . . and so on, along the length of the wood.

Finally, having selected the six best bears, rub the spigot ends down to a slightly concave, smooth finish so that they stand up.

While the lathe is at hand, mount a piece of 1-x-1-inch-square wood in the chuck (we used jelutong), and turn off the two little dome shapes that go to make the headlamps.

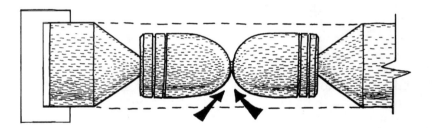

Assembly   Label one face of the chassis "top," and set it top-side-down on the worksurface. Use the pencil, ruler, and square to draw in the two wheel-to-wheel centerlines on the underside.

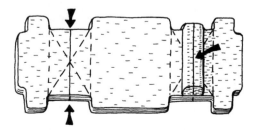

Next, take the 1¼-inch-wide slice from the end of a ¾-inch-thick, 6-inch-wide plank (the wood for the axle-wheel blocks), and cut it in half so that you have two 3-inch lengths at ¾ inch thick and 1¼ inches wide. It's important for screw-fixing the wheels that the grain runs across the thickness of the wood, rather than along its length. Pencil in end-to-end centerlines, and have a trial fitting on the underside of the chassis.

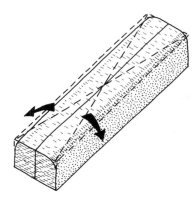

When you are happy with the fit, round off sharp edges and corners. Spread Super Glue 3 on mating surfaces, and set the two blocks in place so that they are centered and in alignment with the wheel-to-wheel centerlines.

Turn the chassis top-side-up, and cut the 10-inch length of ¾-x-½-inch section wood to size so that you have two lengths at 4½ inches. Stick these pieces in place across the top of the chassis so that they run side-to-side at either side of the back wheel recess.

Now, working from front to back along the chassis, glue-fix all the components in place: the hood, the wheel mudguards, the cab, and the truck bed. Screw-fix the wheels to the ends of the axle-wheel blocks, and screw the lamps to the side of the hood. Have a screw and washer on each side of the cab for the door handle, and a screw and nut on the front end of the hood for the radiator cap.

Take teddies a piece at a time and cut ⅛-inch-wide slots into the top of their heads. Have the slot running with the grain.

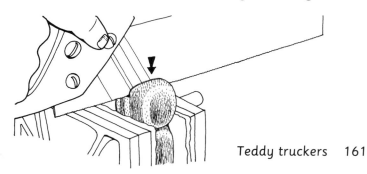

Cut and fit the plywood ears in place. The easiest way to make the ears is to fit a piece of scrap ply in a slot, and draw the ear shapes as shown. Then remove the ply, cut out the shape, glue-fix the two-ear unit in the slot, and rub down to a smooth finish.

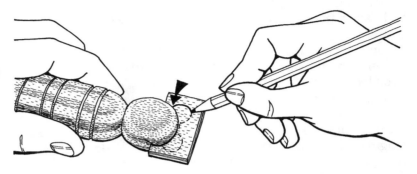

Painting & finishing

When you are happy with the fit and finish of the various blocks and fixings that make up the truck, remove all the screws and the wheels and put them to one side. This done, move the truck to the dust-free area that you have set aside for painting. Have a look at the painting grid on page 163, and arrange all your paints and brushes so that they are close to hand.

Start by painting the chassis black: the underside, the edges, the running board, and the under-bed area. Wait until the paint is touch-dry and loosely screw-fix the four wheels. Next, paint the cab green and the truck bed bright red. It's a good idea to slide a sheet of paper between the cab and the truck.

When the paint is dry, use the pencil and ruler to draw in the shape of the windows on the cab. Now paint the windows black, using the fine-point brush to define the edges, and then block-in with the broad point.

When you are ready to paint the teddy truckers, stand them upright on the worksurface and pick out all the little details that make up the design: the fine features and the bands of color around the bodies. Note how we have given the individual bears slightly different characters: happy, sad, messy, and so on.

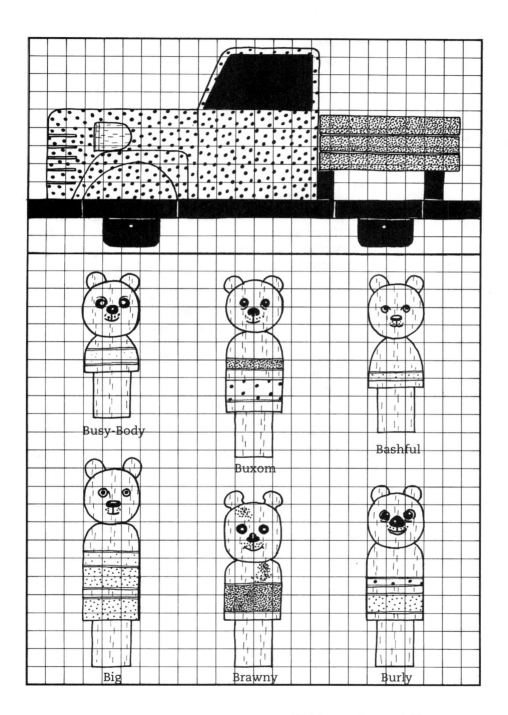

Busy-Body

Buxom

Bashful

Big

Brawny

Burly

Teddy truckers   163

Finally, when the acrylic paints are completely dry, give the whole toy a couple of all-over coats of clear, high-shine varnish (the bears, the truck, and the headlamps), and replace all the screws and fittings. Now the teddy truckers can go off for their picnic!

Special tips

- If you can't use a four-jaw chuck, or if you only have a very small lathe, then you will have to turn single teddies between centers, or turn maybe three teddies at a time and part them off from each other with a saw.
- This is one of those beautiful projects where it doesn't matter too much if the various forms are different from the working drawings. If you want to make a much larger truck, or if you want only a couple of large teddies, or whatever, the design is flexible enough to allow for such modifications.
- Half the secret of successful woodturning is using the correct wood. We like beech, lime, American southern yellow pine, and jelutong. Don't be tempted to use a ragged wood like spruce. If in doubt, ask a specialist supplier.
- Woodturning is potentially very dangerous, especially if there are sudden and unexpected interruptions, so it's best to let friends and family know what you are doing (see lathe checklist in glossary).
- If you like the idea of making the truck but are not so keen on the woodturning, you could whittle the teddies from a length of 1-inch-diameter broomstick dowel.
- In many instances, Super Glue makes such a strong joint/fix on flat mating surfaces that you can do without the screws.

Uncle Sam
Banker Bear

UNCLE SAM BANKER BEAR dressed up in his patriotic Sunday-best clothes—a pair of red-and-white-striped trousers, a blue-tailed coat, and a top hat. Uncle Sam and Baby Bear were busy collecting money for charity. "What I'll do," said Banker Bear to Baby Bear, "is to be friendly and raise my hat and nod my head whenever people put money in the box!"

But—oh, dear!—very soon, the money started to pour in and Banker Bear was taking off his hat and nodding his head as fast as he could. Phew! Banker Bear was very tired and very happy when the box was full; he and Baby Bear could at last stop for a break.

> Uncle Sam Banker Bear,
> Loves his bread and honey,
> But what he likes most of all,
> Is lots of lovely money!
>
> Up and down, up and down,
> It's very, very funny,
> Watching Uncle Sam
> Saying, "Thank you for the money!"

Uncle Sam Banker Bear is an automaton money box. When the lever is pushed down, the coin falls through the slot and Uncle Sam Bear raises his hat and nods his head. Making this project involves the use of a scroll saw, drill, plane, and knife. You will need multicore plywood, jelutong, and dowel rod as you practice the techniques of fretting, box-making, drilling, whittling, and painting.

Materials
Easy-to-carve wood (we recommend lime or jelutong):
    4½" length, about 2" wide × 1½" thick for Sam Bear's body
    A few scraps for the two arms, the head, & the hat
    A block about 2"×2"×3" for Baby Bear
Best-quality multicore plywood
    ½" thick at 12"×8" for the top and bottom of the box
    ¼" at 8"×13" for the sides of the box
14" length of ½-radius quadrant to strengthen the inside corners
    of the box

PROJECT 13

7" length of ¾" to 1"-diameter broomstick dowel for the
    driveshaft
12" length of ¼"-diameter dowel for the levers
Roll of clear, sticky tape
Workout & tracing paper
Eight 1"-long brass countersunk screws
One brass screw eye
Lightweight tension "pulling" spring (you could even use a
    heavy-duty elastic band)
One package of ½" long panel pins or brads
Graded sandpapers
Small amount of Loctite Super Glue 3
Acrylic paint in red, white, dark blue, & pale blue
Small can of high-gloss varnish
Roll of fine, strong twine
2" length of ¼"-wide red satin ribbon

Electric scroll saw   **Tools**
Bench hook
Small tenon saw
Small hand plane
Couple of sharp knives (we used a penknife & a scalpel); they
    must both be razor-sharp
Bench drill & a hand drill, with a good selection of drill bits
Pencil
Ruler
Try square
Screwdriver
Small pin hammer
Bench with a vise

Uncle Sam Bear is an automaton—or, as the dictionary so nicely   **Looking &**
puts it, "a mechanical device operating under its own hidden   **planning**
power." This particular automaton is a sort of hybrid between a
marionette and a walking doll. It really is a delightful and
wonderfully intriguing desk-type toy. Put a coin in the slot, pull
down on the lever, and the little figure nods his head and raises
his hat, and the coin drops into the box. The movement is
ingeniously simple: When the lever is pulled down, a string-
operated, spring-controlled seesaw action takes place, which in
turn sets off the head and arm secondary levers. Magic!

Uncle Sam Banker Bear   167

Before you do anything else, have a good long look at the working drawing on page 169 and the other illustrations, and note the way Uncle Sam Bear has been cut out, sliced down into layers, fretted, glued back together again, whittled, and then fitted with the pivoted arm and head and the strings. Note especially how the middle layer has been cut away to make the string, arm, and neck channels.

If you have any doubts at all as to how such and such a part or piece needs to be cut or fitted, then make a working model or prototype using bits of card and scrap wood. Finally, note how the box is a very simple butt-jointed and pinned construction.

Skill level

Although at first sight this project looks to be quite complex, it is in fact surprisingly straightforward and direct. Certainly, the two primary techniques are a little finger-twisting—the box making and the whittling—but for all that, the overall project is relatively easy. That said, it is vital that you use an easy-to-carve, tight-grained, knot-free wood like lime or jelutong for the figures, and a very sharp knife for the whittling. The most difficult part to carve is the neck and shoulder of the big bear; both the arm and the head need to be able to move freely.

Cutting & carving the bear

When you have a clear understanding of how the whole project needs to be worked and put together, draw Uncle Sam up to full size. Follow the pattern on the top of the illustration, and label the three profiles "front," "side," and "back" shown on page 170.

Next, trace off the three profile views and carefully press-transfer the front and side views through to faces of your chosen wood. Run the wood through the scroll saw and cut away the waste as seen in the front view. Then strap the wood up with sticky tape, and cut out the profile as seen in the side view. When both profile views have been cut out, peel off all the tape so that the waste falls away, leaving you with the square-cornered figure.

Having carefully marked in the middle "string channel" layer, support the figure on the waste back. Run the figure through the saw and cut it down into three slices, as shown. Take the middle slice, mark in the position of the string channel, and cut away the waste. Be sure to leave the back of the collar.

168   *Teddy Bear Treasures*

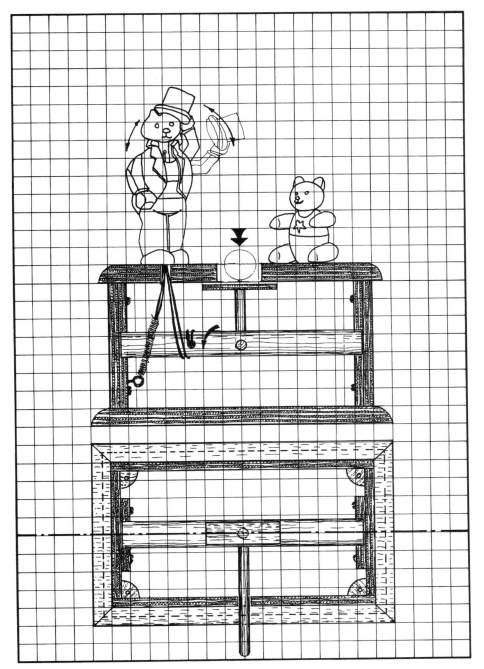

Scale: 2 grid
squares=1 inch

Uncle Sam Banker Bear   169

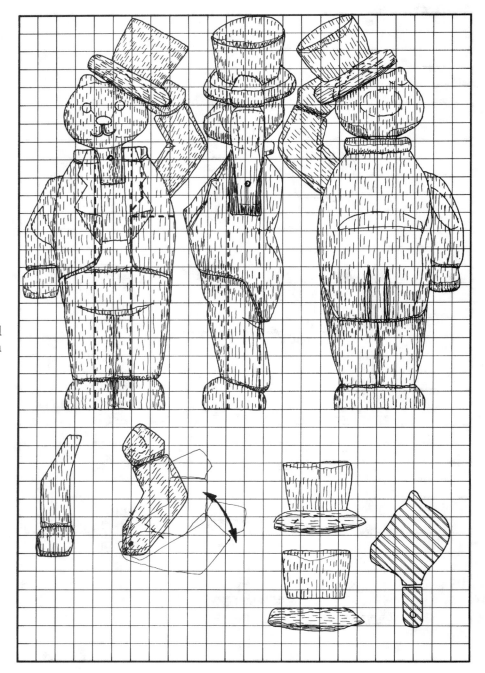

Scale: 4 grid
squares=1 inch

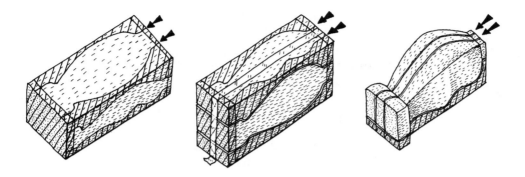

Aiming for a top-to-toe central channel at about ¼ to ½ inch wide, take the raised-arm side and, being very careful not to cut away the collar, cut an arm string channel at about ⅛ to ¼ inch wide.

When you are happy that the channels have been cut as described, take the three body slices, dribble a generous amount of Super Glue on mating faces, and reassemble the layers so as to rebuild the total body form as shown. When the glue is set, pencil-press transfer the profile images through to the wood.

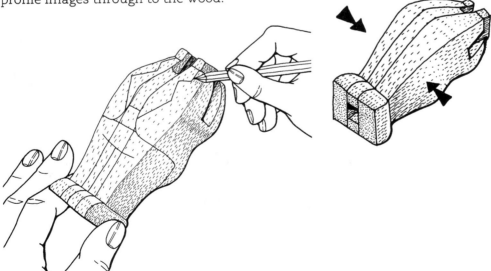

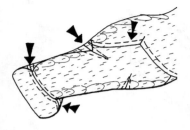

Next, get out the knives and whittle the body form. Aim for a chunky, compact, rounded shape—a form that is stylized and uncomplicated. Make stop-cuts at stepped areas to help define the shapes: around the jacket edges and between the legs and the belt.

Having achieved the basic body shape, take your sharpest knife (we used a little penknife), and cut in the details of coat lapels, shirt front, etc. Again, don't try for realistic details. It's much better to go for strong, chunky forms.

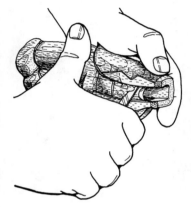

When you come to working the head, hat, and arms, draw the profiles out onto the wood and repeat the carving procedures as already described—only this time, of course, you might well need to keep revising and modifying the shapes one with another so that they all come together for a good fit. NOTE: If you build up the hat from two pieces of wood, then you can prevent the brim being short-grained and fragile.

Finally, use the scalpel to clean out crevices and use sandpaper to tidy up rough areas. Be careful not to blur the desirable, clean-cut knife marks.

Bear assembly

When you have achieved the five elements that make up Uncle Sam Bear (the body, the head, the hat, and the two arms), then comes the tricky, finger-twisting business of putting it all together. First use your finest drill bit to bore out the pivot and string holes. Both the neck and arm need to have side-to-side holes for the pivot and a front-to-back hole for the string.

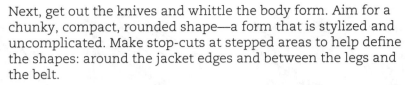

Take two 18-inch lengths of fine, strong twine, and thread them through the neck and arm cord holes, and knot them off at either side of the wood/hole, so that there is about 9 inches of cord hanging down from each side of the neck and from each side of the arm.

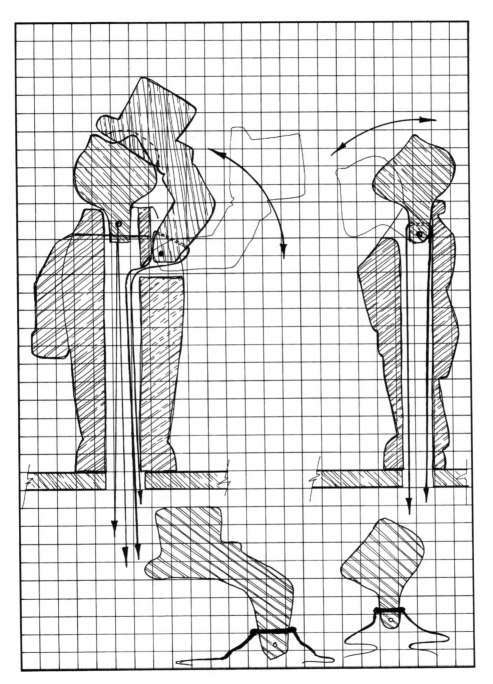

Scale: 4 grid
squares=1 inch

Thread the two head cords down through the body of the bear, and pivot the neck by pushing a pin through the side collar, the neck, and out through the other side collar. Note that you might need to trim up the neck socket and/or the actual neck until the head is an easy swing fit.

Fit-and-fix the arm in like manner, with the pivot running from the front to the back of the shoulder. Cut a notch in the brim of the hat, and glue-fit the top hat to the hand so that when the arm is in the at-rest, raised position, the hat comes up against the head so as to cover one ear. Next, carve, fit, and glue-fix the right arm to the side of the body.

Now, if all is well, there should be a total of four cords coming out from under the bear. Divide them into two groups of two, and label them with masking tape labels, "up" and "down" accordingly. When you pull on the two down cords, the head and the arm should swing down, and when you pull on the up cords the head and the arm swing back up.

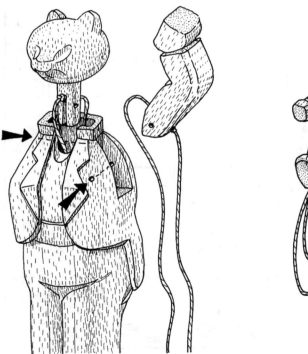
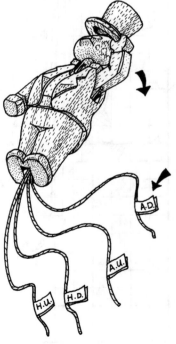

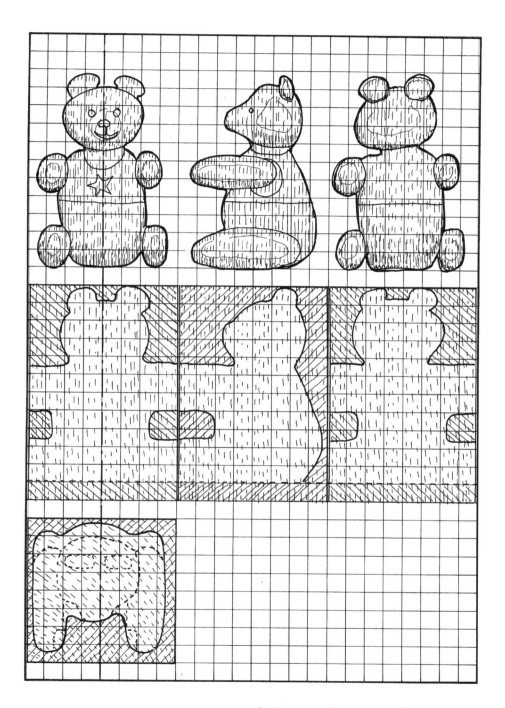

Uncle Sam Banker Bear   175

Making the baby bear

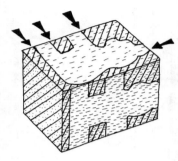

Draw the baby bear out to full size, following the pattern on the top of page 175. Make a clear tracing; then take the block of wood and pencil-press transfer the profiles through to the sides. Make sure that, from one side face of the block to another, the bear profiles all relate to the same head and baseline. Shade in the areas of waste.

When the wood is set out with the profiles, then repeat the scroll-saw-cutting procedure as described for the large bear: Cut out one profile, strap the waste back in place, and cut out the other profile, and so on. With Baby Bear, you will be able to take this procedure a little further, and cut away the waste as seen in top view.

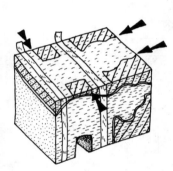

When you have removed all the waste and achieved a square-cut bear, take the knife and whittle the form to a rounded finish. It's all straightforward enough, as long as you don't force the pace by cutting too deeply and splitting the wood. NOTE: Because the arms and legs are relatively fragile in that the grain runs from across the limbs through the block, you will need to support the limbs throughout the carving process.

The ears should be modeled so that they taper towards the tips. Finally, when you have whittled the bear to shape, take the sandpaper and rub the whole thing down to a nicely rounded, good-to-hold finish.

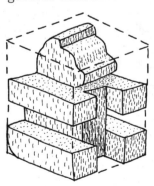
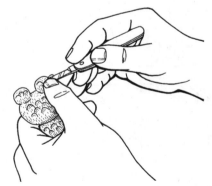

Building the box

Having studied the design template shown on page 177, take the ¼-inch-thick multicore plywood, and use the square, measure, and pencil to set out the four sides that make up the

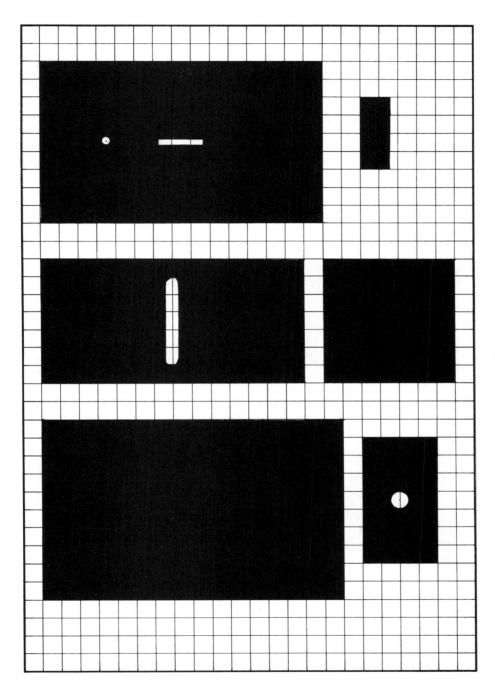

Scale: 4 grid
squares=1 inch

Uncle Sam Banker Bear   177

box. You need two long sides each measuring 7×3½ inches, and two ends each measuring 3½×3 inches.

Next, take the ½-inch-thick plywood, and set out two rectangles—the box top at 4¼ × 7½ inches, and the bottom at 8 × 5 inches. It's most important that all the corners are carefully set out so that they are as near as possible perfect right angles, so take time getting it just right.

Now, having used the tenon saw as shown, to cut out the six panels (the four sides, and the top and the bottom), take the plane and carefully round-over the top edges of the top and bottom of the box. Try to achieve a smooth ½-inch radius curve.

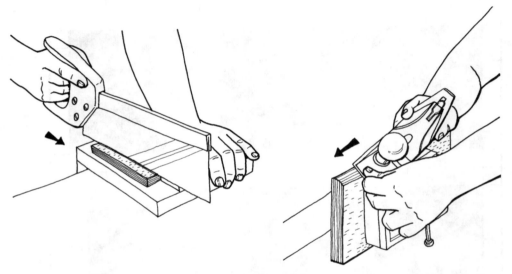

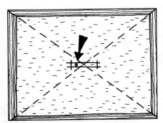

Having noted how the 1¼-inch-long, ¼-inch-wide coin slot is centered on top of the box lid/top, drill a pilot hole for the scroll saw. Unhitch the saw blade and pass it through the hole. Then retension the blade, and cut the slot to size as described in other projects (See Betty Bear, the nursery clock, project 8). Repeat this slot-cutting procedure for the lever slot on the front side of the box.

When you are happy with the slots, take the ½-inch-radius quadrant, and cut it into four 3½-inch lengths. Sand all the parts to a smooth finish. Have a look back at the working

178   Teddy Bear Treasures

drawing to see how the sides are butted up against the ends and the corners strengthened with the strips of quadrant. Then glue and pin the box sides together accordingly. Drive the pins below the surface of the wood, fill, and sand to a good finish.

When you have achieved the box sides, all true and square, set the top and the bottom of the box in place, and fit and fix with a countersunk screw at each corner—one into each corner quadrant.

Having made Sam Bear, Baby Bear, and the box, remove the bottom of the box, and cut and drill the two driveshaft plates, one at each end of the box. Trial fit the ¾- to 1-inch-diameter driveshaft. The shaft needs to be a nice, easy, contained fit within the box.

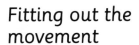

Fitting out the movement

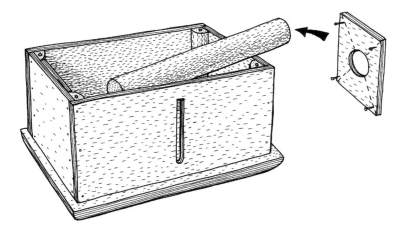

Having removed the shaft and established the position of Uncle Sam, run a ¼-inch-diameter hole through the top of the box, and glue and screw-fix him in place on the box and over the hole. Glue-fix Baby Bear in place.

Measure halfway along the shaft, and mark out the position of the two ¼-inch dowels. Drill a ¼-inch-diameter hole through the shaft, and fit and fix the lever dowel in place. Next, using a scrap of ⅝-inch wood as a jig, drill out the ¼-inch-diameter coin slot dowel hole. Reckon on the coin slot dowel plus the plywood

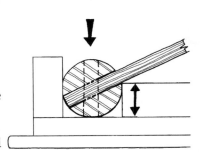

Uncle Sam Banker Bear   179

coin stop being long enough to come within ⅛ inch of the underside of the coin slot.

Fit, fix, and glue the dowels and the coin stop in place. Put the box on its side and fix one driveshaft plate in place. Now slide the other plate on the driveshaft, arrange and slot the driveshaft in the box and fit the other plate.

With the lever on the box in the up position, gather the two "down" cords—one for the arm and one for the head. Knot them together, wrap them once around the driveshaft, and fix the knotted end to the shaft with a pin or screw. See working drawing on page 181.

Next, run a screw-eye into the inside of the box at a point somewhere below Uncle Sam and near the bottom of the box. Now for the most difficult bit of all: Fit the two "up" cords, via the spring, to the screw-eye. If all is well, when you press down on the trip-lever, Uncle Sam's arm and the head should swing down. When you release the lever, the arm and the head should be pulled back in place by the spring. Be warned: Fitting the string and the spring is one of those tasks that requires a deal of fiddling about before things work out.

Finally, when all the movements have been strung, sprung, and knotted and all the knots have been sealed and clinched with Super Glue, then the bottom of the box can be screwed back into place. NOTE: Be careful to support the box so that the teddies are protected.

Painting

Fill and rub the whole workpiece down to a good finish. Clean up all the dust and debris, and move to the dust-free area that you have set aside for painting. Now comes the very exciting task of painting. Before you begin, study the painting grid.

If you want to go for more personalized imagery such as names, dates, special patterns, or different color details for the costumes, then now is the time to think it through. Prior to painting the box, place it on a piece of scrap wood so that the painted base and edges are clear of the worksurface, and wedge the lever and teddy's arm in the halfway-up position.

Uncle Sam Banker Bear   181

Start by laying on the main areas of ground color: pale blue for the box, dark blue for Uncle Sam's coat, white for his trousers, shirt and hat, and red for the Baby Bear's vest. You might need to sand and apply a second coat. When the ground colors are dry, then pencil-press transfer the swag details through to the side of the box, and pencil in all the guidelines on the two bears; the stripes on the trousers, waistband, and hat; and the two stars—one on Baby Bear's vest and the other on the hat.

When you are happy with the overall effect, and when the acrylic paints are completely dry, then give the whole workpiece—the box, the bears, and the lever—a couple of coats of clear, high-shine varnish. When the varnish is dry, fold the ¼-inch-wide ribbon in half and glue-fix it over the neck area to cover the pull-cord. And now, finally, Banker Bear and Baby Bear are ready to take your money!

Special tips
- If you like the idea of the project but are not so keen on the idea of making the box, you could consider using a ready-made box. If you do use such a box, then you will have to adjust the various working and decorative details to fit.
- Remember that the box needs to have a screw-fitted base so that you can take the money out!
- One of the joys of a project of this type and character is the fact that you can change just about everything to suit your own design needs. You could make a large lady bear, or a group of bears, or the Baby Bear could nod his head. And then again, you could even change the theme and introduce a little car, or period dress, or figures to illustrate a story, or whatever takes your fancy.
- Don't be tempted to use a fancy wood for the bears, such as yellow pine. It's most important that you use an easy-to-carve wood. I would go for a bland variety like lime or jelutong.
- The putting-together stages (fitting the strings and getting the arms and the hat to spring back into place) are somewhat tricky and finger-twisting. This being so, you might well ask a small-fingered friend to help you out.

Bonny Bear speedster

BONNY BEAR loved her white Fleetwood Sixty Special Cadillac Convertible more than anything else in the whole wide world. She polished it after breakfast, she polished after lunch, and she polished it after dinner. It was just about the cleanest, shiniest car that you ever did see. And, of course, Bonnie was a very careful driver. When Bonny Bear was at the wheel, she looked left and then right, and then left and then right, and then left . . .

> Cruising along in her Fleetwood Convertible
> Chasing along in her white Cadillac
> Cheerful Bonny in her Sixty Special
> Speeding there, and zooming back!
>
> Driving along in her Fleetwood Caddy
> Coasting along in her car all white
> Driving across the bedroom carpet
> Look to the left, and look to the right.

This toy car is a likeness of a Cadillac 1959 Fleetwood Special. The bear has a crank-operated side-to-side head movement. In making this project, you will utilize your lathe, scroll saw, drill, and Surform rasps while making use of multicore plywood, American southern yellow pine and jelutong. The project's techniques include turning, fretting, shaping, gluing, and painting.

Materials

Multicore birch plywood
   ¾"-thick at 4"×8" for the chassis base
   ¼"-thick at about 12"×18" for all the layers that make up the car body, and for the under-axle plate
16" length of 3"×3" jelutong for the hood, the trunk, the five wheels and teddy's hat
15" length of 2½"×2½" sectioned American southern yellow pine for the teddy bear
Workout & tracing paper
6" length of ½" diameter dowel for the neck/drive shaft
Graded sandpapers
Four brass/chrome round-head screws with washers to fit for the arms, steering wheel and spare wheel
Six brass countersink screws for the chassis

Four large screw-eyes with four brass washers to fit
Washer large enough to slide over the ½" diameter drive shaft
Two 6" lengths of ⅛"-diameter coat-hanger wire
Super Glue
Acrylic paints in red, black, & white
Clear, high-shine varnish

Lathe with a four-jaw chuck to fit
Good selection of turning tools, to include a small round-nosed gouge & a skew chisel
Compass
Dividers
Calipers
Straight saw
Small rasp
Electric scroll saw (we used a Draper scroll saw)
Coping saw with a pack of fine blades
Selection of chisels and gouges (We used a shallow curve ³⁄₁₆" gouge, a ⅛" chisel, & a ⅛" spoon gouge.)
Pencil
Ruler
Try square
Drill with a good selection of bits to fit sizes ranging from ⅛" to 1¼" diameter
Soft-haired paintbrushes, fine & broad

Looking & planning

If you enjoy turning, if you know of a child who likes automobiles, and if you are looking to make a really exciting push-around-the-floor action toy, this project is the one for you. The car is a beauty!

Have a good long look at the working drawings on page 186. The scale is 2 grid squares to 1 inch, and the toy stands at about 7 inches high, 5½ inches wide, and 9 inches long. Study the construction details, and note how the toy is made and put together.

The chassis slab is made from ¾-inch-thick plywood, the body panels of the car are laminated up from ¼-inch-thick ply, while all the other components—the hood, the trunk, and all the bits

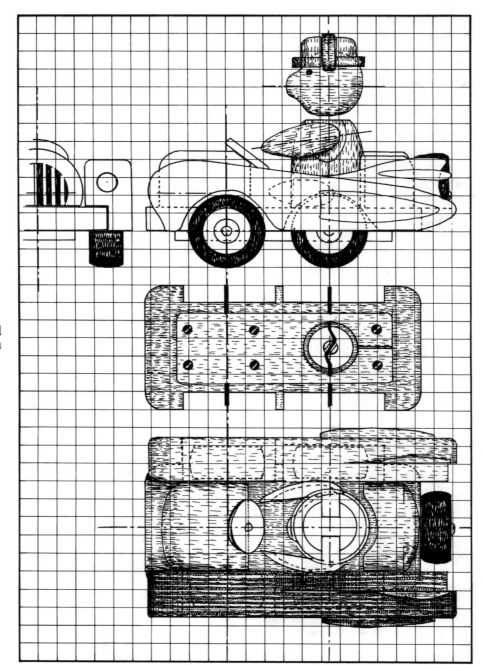

Scale: 2 grid
squares=1 inch

that make up the bear—are turned on the lathe. Note the two coat-hanger-wire axle rods, and the way the back axle has a Z-crank.

Have a close-up look at the details and sections, and see how the Z-crank locates in the slotted bottom of the through-body neck dowel shaft, resulting in a reciprocating or side-to-side movement of the head. The drive mechanism is delightfully simple and direct. In use, the fixed wheels rotate the back axle, the rotating axle sets the curious Z-crank in motion, the crank joggles and twists the vertical through-body drive shaft, and the shaft sets the bear's head turning slowly from side to side.

The bear is made up from seven turnings: The head, the hat, a dome-topped cylinder for the body, two little discs for the ears, and two sausage spindles for the limbs. When you are ready to make the legs and arms, all you do is to split the two spindles lengthwise (we used a Draper saw) and glue and screw the resultant flat-faced forms to the side of the body.

The car is pretty straightforward—a plywood chassis, a couple of dome-top turnings for the hood and the trunk, five turned wheels, and the laminated side panels. Have a look at the working drawings, and see how the beautifully sculpted body panels are made by first gluing together a number of thin plywood cutouts, and then by shaping the resultant laminated forms with a rasp and sandpaper.

Skill level

This project is easier than it looks! If you study the working drawings carefully and tackle the making stages one step at a time, it is pretty straightforward. That said, you need to take extra care to get the head movement to work smoothly.

Roughing out

When you have studied the project details and drawn the various shapes and designs up to full size, pin all the designs and drawings up on the wall, and clear the workshop ready for action.

Take the 16-inch length of 3-x-3-inch-square section jelutong and check it over to make sure that it is free from splits, dead knots, stains, and waney edges. Find the end-centers by drawing crossed diagonals on the square-cut ends of the wood.

Set the compass/dividers to a radius of 1½ inches, and inscribe the ends of the wood with 3-inch-diameter circles. Mark off pencil tangents at the diagonal-to-circle intersections (the crossover points) and establish the areas of waste by drawing lines from the resultant octagons down the length of the wood. Take your plane, rasp or drawknife, and swiftly clear away the waste until the wood is more or less octagonal in section (see *roughing out* in glossary).

Punch in center marks at both ends of the wood. Position and clamp one end in the chuck, and then secure the work by running the tailstock center tightly into the wood. If you are using a dead center, ease back the tailstock a fraction and dribble a little oil into the spin hole. Position the tool rest so that it is as close as possible to the work and just a little below the centerline.

Set out all your tools so that they are comfortably at hand, and make sure that you and the lathe are in good order (see *lathe checklist* in glossary), and turn on the lathe. Take the tool of your choice (we used a large, round-nosed gouge), and start by making a few practice runs up and down the wood, just to get the feel of your tool and the wood. Finally, swiftly turn the wood down to a cylinder.

Turning the profiles

When you have turned off the rough, set the calipers to 2½ inches and turn the wood down to a smooth 2½-inch-diameter cylinder. Take your pencil, ruler, and dividers and mark all the stepoffs that make up the design of the various turnings. Working from left to right along the spinning wood and following the illustration shown, mark off the following:

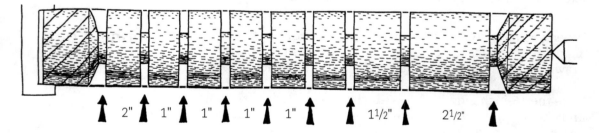

2"   1"   1"   1"   1"   1½"   2½"

- 2 inches for chuck waste
- 1 inch for each of the four road wheels and the spare, with ¼ inch of waste in between each wheel
- 1 inch for the hat
- ¼ inch for waste
- 1½ inch for the trunk
- ¼ inch for waste
- 2½ inches for the hood/engine block
- the remainder for waste

When you have stepped off along the cylinder all the widths, then take the parting tool and the skew chisel and sink each of the waste areas in to a depth of ¾ inch. If all is well, you should be left with a 1-inch-diameter central core.

Next, with the calipers and the gouge, turn each of the stepoffs down to the required diameter. From left to right, the finished sizes need to be set at:

- 2-inch diameter for each of the wheels
- a little under 2 inches for the hat brim
- 1½-inch diameter for the hat crown
- 2½-inch diameter for the hood
- 2½ inches for the trunk

Check the measurements carefully because there's no going back once you have removed the wood.

When you are happy that all is correct, take the skew chisel and, working from high to low, turn off the sharp shoulders and work towards the desired forms. When you have turned down all the curves—the edges of the wheels and the rounded

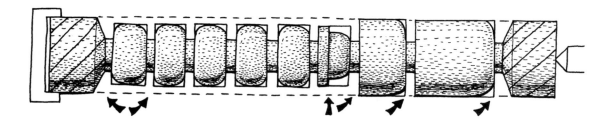

Bonny Bear speedster   189

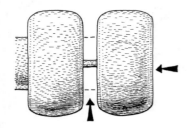

shapes at the ends of the hood and the trunk, and the rounded crown of the hat—hone the skew chisel to a razor sharpness and turn the wood to a fine finish. Hopefully, you won't need sandpaper, but just in case you do, settle for a swift rubbing-down with the finest grade, being all the while very careful that you don't overdo the sanding and blur the crisp shapes.

Finally, when you have achieved all the dips, sweeps, and curves that make up the various forms, wind the tailstock out of the way, and work along the turning from the tailstock end back towards the headstock, parting off the separate components and bringing the end faces to a good finish. NOTE: The wheels need to have whitewall and hub rings on one side.

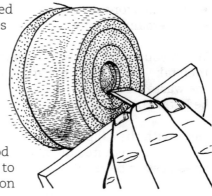

Turning & fitting the bear

When you have studied the illustration on page 191, mount the southern yellow pine on the lathe and repeat the turning procedure as already described. This time, of course, turn off the six components that make up the bear: the head, the dome-topped body, the two sausage-like limb turnings, and the two little discs that will become the ears. Bring the various components to a good finish and part off (see top of illustration, page 191.)

Being very careful that you don't make a mess-up of the wood or your fingertips, run the arm and leg turnings end-to-end through the scroll saw so as to split them in half along their length. There's no easy way to do this. You could make a pair of side-gripping V-block cradles/jigs to hold the wood while it is being sawn, but really it's best to pencil in the line of cut and then run the wood through the saw and cut by eye. The safest procedure is to push the workpiece halfway through, and then change ends and draw it the rest of the way through. It is a little bit tricky, so take your time. See to it that the wood is well supported, and make sure that your attention doesn't wander.

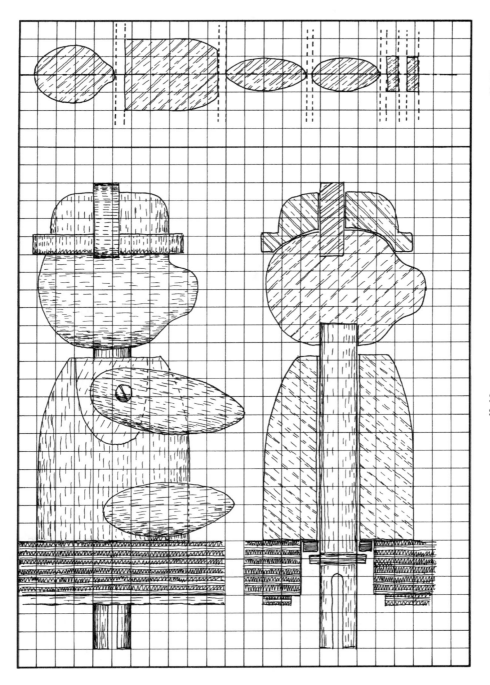

Scale: 2 grid
squares=1 inch

Scale: 4 grid
squares=1 inch

Bonny Bear speedster 191

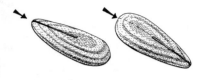

NOTE: If you are at all nervous, support the turnings in a rag-muffled vise and cut them in half with a small, flat saw like a gents or a tenon.

When you have cut the two little turnings down into four flat-faced half-spindles—a pair for the legs and a pair for the arms—pin a sheet of sandpaper sand-side-up on the worksurface and rub the sawn faces down to a smooth finish.

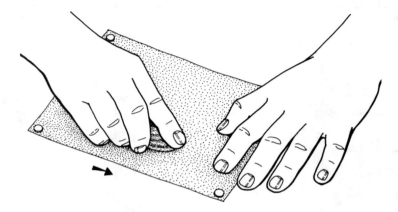

Take the body turning, swiftly rub the base down to a level finish, and mark in the top-center point. This done, take the drill and the ⅝-inch bit, and run a hole straight down through the turning. While the drill is at hand, drill a ¼-inch-deep, ½-inch-diameter hole in the neck side of the head for the driveshaft dowel.

Fitting the ears is a bit finger-twisting, so be warned. It requires a straight eye and steady hands. First, mark in on the turned head the position of the neck dowel, the eyes, the nose, and, of course, the two ears. As the ears are a little over ¼ inch thick and about 1 inch in diameter, aim to sink them into the head to a depth of about ⅜ inch. You won't go far wrong if you figure on the slots being about ¾ to ⅞ inch long.

Mark the ears "left" and "right," and then, just as you might cut a mortise or maybe a housing slot, use the saw and a small chisel to scoop out the little part-disc holes. Support the head in one hand, hold the chisel as you might hold a pen or a probing instrument, and remove the waste with little scooping cuts (see *ear slots* in glossary and project 9). Having carefully fitted each ear, use a scroll saw to cut the hat to slot and fit over the ears.

Finally, having used a chisel and sandpaper to cut flat-faced limb seatings on each side of the body, fix the bear's arms and legs in place; glue the legs and drill and screw the arms.

First cut the ¾-inch base chassis slab to size, following the middle pattern in the illustration on page 186. Use the compass to mark in the quarter-circle corners, and then use a scroll saw to remove the waste. This done, draw in an end-to-end centerline, and mark in the position of the hood and trunk, the through-body Z-crank hole, and the axle slots.

Now, have a look at the illustration, and see how the hood/engine block and trunk turnings need to be sliced along their length (about ½ inch below the centerline) so as to give them a flat base. See also how a slice is taken off for the steering wheel seating, and a scoop is taken off for the back-of-bear seat rest.

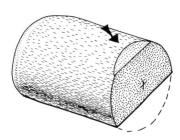

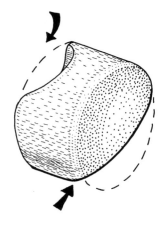

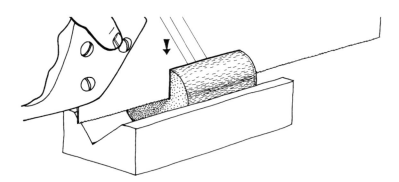

It's all pretty straightforward. When you come to cutting the seat rest scoop, best support the wood end-up in the jaws of a vise and clear away the waste with a scoop gouge and a Surform rasp. Aim for an easy, wraparound, smooth-curved form that reflects the shape of the bear's body. Finally, when you have cut the hood and the trunk to size and shape and sanded to a good finish, and when you are happy that all is

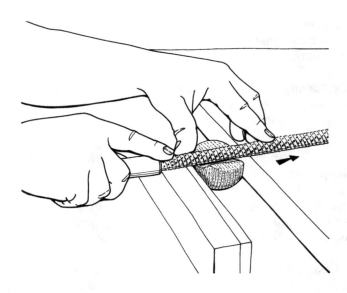

well, set the two shapes down on the chassis slab in alignment with the various guidelines, and use a pencil to establish registration marks.

Making the side panels

First have another look at the working drawing on page 195 and the design template. Note how the two side panels are made up from 10¼-inch-thick fretted plywood components: five for each panel. See also how within each five-layer panel, and from the outer face of the panel through to the inside-near-chassis face, the sandwich or lay-up order of the cutouts is: a single one-wheel arch profile, two two-wheel arch profiles, and two tailfin profiles.

When you have a clear understanding of how the plywood layers are sandwiched together, draw the panels to full size, take a tracing, and then carefully pencil-press transfer the traced lines through to the plywood. This done, run the wood through the scroll saw and fret out the profiles. Arrange the cutouts in order, five for each side of the car. Check several times to make sure that the order is correct, and then laminate the layers together with the Super Glue.

Scale: 2 grid
squares=1 inch

Bonny Bear speedster   195

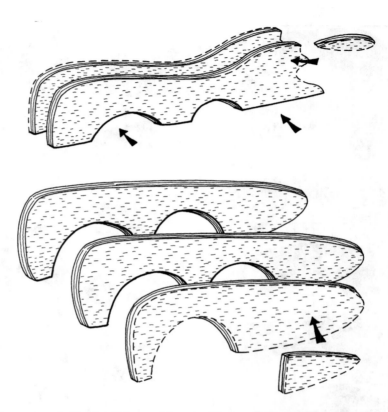

Be warned: You need two identical but mirror-imaged car sides, so spend time getting it right.

While the saw is at hand, fret out the small trim details: the two side vents and the rocket-fin lights, the under-axle panel, and the steering wheel. Sand to a good finish.

When you have achieved the two panels and glue-fixed the little bits of trim (the rocket-fin lights and the vents), then comes the slow and painstaking task of rounding off the various edge curves that make up the design. If you have any doubts as to how the shapes need to be, then it's a good idea to make a Plasticine working model or maquette.

The working procedure is simple enough. Once you have identified the areas that need to be cut away, you simply reduce the waste with the rasp and the sandpaper.

NOTE: Make sure that the workpiece is completely dry before you start sanding. We say this because, in our experience, if the plywood is in any way damp (such as if you have used a lot of water-based glue or have been working in a damp shed), the surface of the ply will feather and fluff up to the extent that it is almost impossible to bring to a good finish.

Finally, when the curves have been rasped to shape, the two sides are nicely matched, and damage has been made good with filler, then rub down with the graded sandpaper until you have two nicely curved side panels.

Set the car hood/engine block, the side panels, the bear's body, and the trunk on the chassis slab, and ease them around for best fit. Recheck lines and draw new lines where necessary. Take the drill and the ⅛- to ³⁄₁₆-inch bit and run screw-fixing holes through the chassis slab. Reckon on having two screws for each of the three components: the hood, the trunk, and the bear.

Working the chassis

Note how the two bear-fixing screws occur in the axle housing channel. Run a pilot hole through the marked out crank circle and use either a large machine-bit drill or the scroll saw to clear away the waste. The hole needs to be big enough to allow the crank to turn, and yet smaller than the base of the bear. Aim for a hole diameter of about 1¼ inches.

Set the chassis slab bottom-up in the vise, and use a saw and a ⅛-inch gouge/chisel to cut the two axle housing channels. Make sure that the back axle channel runs right across the center of the crank hole. Note how the channel needs to be widened slightly on either side of the hole to allow free movement for the crank.

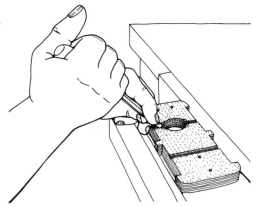

Assembly

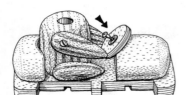

Now comes the tricky but exciting part! When you have cut the axle channels and drilled the various holes, screw the hood, the trunk, and the bear's body into place on the chassis.

Take the steering wheel and use a round-head screw and a brass washer to fix it in position on the angled dashboard as shown. Now carefully pin/screw and glue-fix the car body panels in place at either side of the chassis.

Having glue-fixed the dowel, the ears, and the hat in position, slide the neck shaft down through the body and base. Cut the end of the dowel so that at least ½ inch sticks out and down through the crank hole. Remove the head-and-dowel-shaft unit, mark up about ¾ inch from the bottom of the shaft, and use either the scroll or fretsaw to cut a ⅛-inch-wide, ¾-inch-long crank slot. Mark and drill a ⅛-inch-diameter hole for the through-dowel peg.

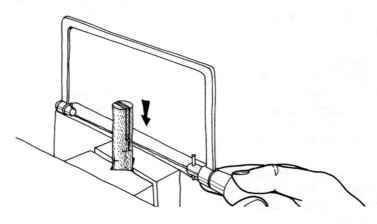

Drill ⅛-inch-diameter axle holes through the back-center of the wheels and run them in to a depth of about ½ inch. With the car set base-up in the vise and supported on waste wood, slide the bear's neck shaft into position and hold it in place with a large brass washer and a wooden peg.

Use a pair of pliers to cut the axle rods to length and to shape the Z-crank. Test the movement of the Z-crank. Flatten the axle ends slightly, smear with glue, and push-fit the wheels on the axles.

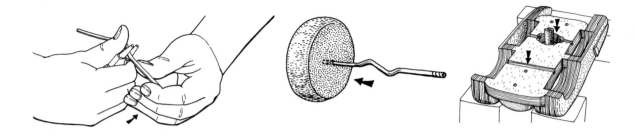

Set the rods down into their channels and screw the plywood base plate into position. Finally, drill and screw-fix the spare wheel to the back end of the trunk.

When the glue is set, and when you have variously adjusted the shaft slot and the shape of the Z-crank so as to achieve an easy and efficient head movement, clean up all the dust and debris and retreat to the area that you have set aside for painting.

Remove the end-of-shaft peg and all the screws, and break the toy down into primary parts. Now, bearing in mind that acrylics become touch-dry in about 15 minutes, study the Painting Grid on page 200. Paint the whole car white—under the chassis, the panels, the hood, and the trunk—all surfaces and edges. If necessary, lay on several coats.

Next paint the steering wheel, the wheel centers, the hat, the under-axle plate, and the bear's vest bright red. When the red is dry, paint the wheel tires and the details of the face black, the tire walls and the spots on the hat and the bow decoration white, and the rocket-fin, other lights, and the radiator grill red.

When the paint is dry, fit-and-fix the bear and the drive shaft back into position, make good scuff marks, and paint in anything else that takes your fancy—a name or number plate, and so on.

Finally, put the car back together. Give the whole workpiece a couple of coats of varnish, fit the pull-cord screw-eyes two at

Painting & finishing

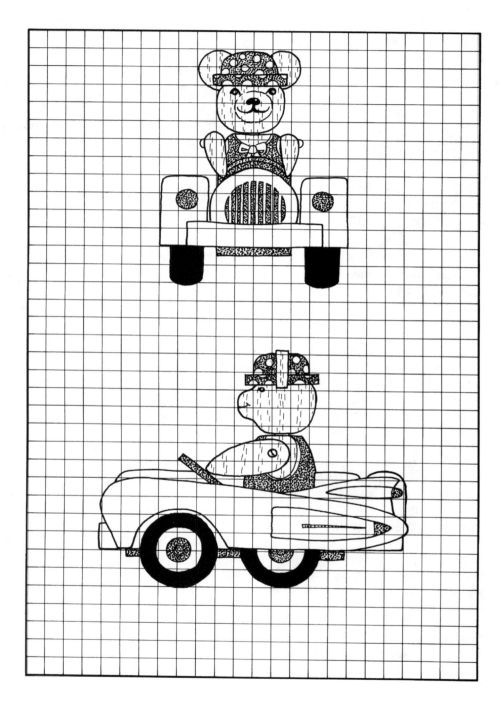

the front and two at the back, and the car is finished and ready for its first *brmmm!* across the highways of the playroom carpet.

- If you have a good-size , solid lathe, then skip the octagonal section bit and turn the square-section wood straight down to a cylinder.
- If you have to turn multiples, say wheels, or pegs or whatever, then it's a good idea to turn a few extras so that you can choose the best-matched group.
- If you are a beginner to turning, it's best to run through a pre-switch-on checklist: Is the lathe in good order? Does the cutout switch operate? Are your sleeves rolled up? Are the tools within reach but out of harm's way? Is the tool rest set correctly? See glossary.
- In the context of toymaking, always make sure that the fixings are safe. Use glue and brass screws or glue and wooden pegs.
- In the context of toymaking, make sure that all the materials are finger-licking toddler-sucking safe. Use nontoxic acrylics rather than oil paints. Never use old household paints. Never use toxic woods like yew, or splintery woods.
- The ¼-inch-thick plywood layers that make up the side panel could be cut out in a stack as 10 identical multiples, and then selected layers could be trimmed back accordingly.

acrylic paint An easy-to-use, water-based, quick-drying, PVA paint. Acrylics are really good for toymaking. They can be used straight from the can, the colors are bright, the brushes can be washed clean in water, and once in place, they are nontoxic. As teddy bear toys get a lot of handling, it's a good idea to protect the painted surfaces with a couple of coats of clear, high-shine varnish.

axle If it supports and pivots a wheel, then it is an axle. In the context of this book, an axle might be anything from a long screw through to a length of dowel. If you are using screws, best use a brass roundhead. Try, if possible, to drive it into side grain rather than end grain.

bearing Any containment—tube, guide, or locating bridge-shaped block—that holds and supports a turning shaft, an axle, or a pivot might be termed a bearing. Mating moving surfaces—where the axle passes through the bearing—are best left in the plain wood state and then waxed.

beech A heavy, pleasant-to-work, yellow-orange, hardwood; perfect for toymaking. Beech turns, saws, and cuts well, and generally takes a good finish. Beech is very useful for making complex profiles and hard-edged details.

bench hook A very useful, easy-to-make sawing aid. In use, it is hooked over the edge of the bench or secured in the vise. The workpiece is butted hard up-against the hook and held with one hand, while the saw is operated with the other hand.

between centers The act or technique of turning the wood to a round section while it is mounted/secured between the forked headstock center/chuck and the pointed tailstock center. See *lathe*.

blank A piece of prepared, ready-to-work wood—a block, slab, disc or cylinder.

brushes We use the same soft-haired brushes—sable or nylon—as are used by watercolor artists. There are flat brushes for varnishing, long-haired fine-point brushes for details, broad brushes for large areas of flat paint, and so on. Wash and dry your brushes as soon as you have finished with them, and store them with the heads tight-bound with plastic film.

butt joint Butt joints are used where two pieces of wood need to be joined flush. Mating faces are glued, butted together face-to-face, and then fixed with pins or screws.

calipers A two-curve-legged measuring instrument, used for checking widths and diameters.

carton card Salvaged cardboard packaging used for making patterns, working models, and templates.

centers In a woodturning context, the forked center at the headstock end of the lathe, and the pointed/cup/live center at the tailstock end are both termed *centers*. If a project describes the technique as, "turning between centers," the workpiece is turned while it is being held and pivoted between the forked drive center and the pointed tailstock center.

centering and roughing out The technique or process of mounting the wood on the lathe and swiftly turning it down to a ready-to-work cylinder. Starting with a square section length of wood, the working stages are:

1. Establish the end centerpoints by drawing crossed diagonals.
2. Locate/spike the wood onto the pronged drive/headstock center.
3. Bring the tailstock up towards the work and clamp it into position.
4. Wind the tailstock center into the wood.
5. Fix the tool rest just below center height so that it is clear of the work, and test for a clear, unobstructed swing.
6. Grasp the tool in both hands and brace it on the rest.
7. Switch on the power and run the tool back and forth along the wood until the initial cylinder is roughed out.

If you are working on a small lathe, the wood is best cut down to an octagonal section, before being mounted on the lathe. See *roughing out*.

centerline In the context of working drawings and setting out the wood, a centerline is one or more lines that mark out the center of a symmetrical form or image. Each working face might have a centerline that runs from side-to-side, another that runs from front-to-back, and so on.

chisels We favor bevel-edged chisels. We generally use four widths: ¼ inch, ½ inch, ¾ inch and 1 inch. It's best to use a chisel width that is slightly narrower than the groove/channel being cut.

chuck (four-jawed chuck) In the context of woodturning on a large lathe, a four-jaw chuck is a beautifully efficient and time-saving piece of equipment that is used to hold and grip the workpiece while it is being turned. In use, the four jaws are screwed, in geared unison, toward the center, so as to grip and centralize the round or square-section workpiece.

clamps Devices used for holding the workpiece secure while it is being worked. There are G-clamps, C-clamps, strap clamps, hold-downs, holdfasts, and so on. In use, the workpiece is best protected by having an offcut waster set between it and the jaws/head of the holdfast/clamp. See *V-block*.

close-grained A term used to describe wood that has regularly spaced annual rings. In the context of small toys that are going to be cuddled and sucked, always make sure that your chosen wood is splinter-proof and nontoxic.

compasses A two-legged handheld instrument used for drawing circles and arcs. We use a long-legged, multipurpose, screw-operated type with a pen-holding attachment and an extension arm. See also *dividers*.

coping saw A small, flexible-bladed frame saw used for cutting curves, holes, and profiles in thin section wood. A good saw for teddy bear toymaking, in that the inexpensive pin-ended blades can be swiftly removed and refitted.

counterbalance Many of the small teddy bear toys use a counterbalance, usually in the form of a see-saw weight or extension to balance and/or offset another movement.

countersink Prior to using a screw, to enlarge the upper part of a hole to make a cone-shaped depression so that the head of the screw can be sunk below the surface.

craft knife A knife with a short, sharp, strong, easy-to-change blade.

crank An off-set bend or kink in a shaft, used to convert rotary motion to reciprocating motion, or vice versa. In the context of small wooden teddy bear toys, cranked axles and handles are used to set some part of the toy in motion.

cutouts The wooden shapes that make up the project; the sawn profiles as they come off the scroll saw/lathe.

designing The process of working out shapes, structures, forms, functions, and details. We usually:

1. Draw inspiration from traditional originals and/or past projects.
2. Modify the size, shape, and imagery to suit our own needs.
3. Make working models from bits of wood, card, string, and Plasticine.
4. Make further modifications and adjustments.
5. Finally, draw up full-size measured designs.

dividers A two-legged compass-like instrument used for stepping off measurements. In the context of woodturning, the heavy-duty knife-point dividers are fixed to a set measurement and held against the workpiece while it is in motion. The points mark the surface with small V-groove cuts. Be warned: Beginners are best advised to stop the lathe when using dividers.

double-sided sticky tape A clear plastic sticky-on-both-sides tape; good for holding pieces of plywood together while cutting out identical multiple shapes on the scroll saw.

dowel Shop-bought, ready-to-use round section wood is one of the toymaker's primary materials. Dowel is sold in diameters that range from ⅛ inch, ¼ inch, ⅜ inch, through to 1 inch. Dowel can be used as axle rods or sliced to make wheels or cut and carved and made into limbs or used for glue-peg fixing, and so on.

drilling holes The act of boring, sinking, or running holes through the workpiece. Depending upon the job in hand, we use variously a hand-held electric drill, a bench or press drill, and a small wind-and-turn hand drill. I prefer to work with a hand-operated drill, because it takes a good range of bit sizes, is silent, is inexpensive, and is totally controllable. In use, the workpiece is backed with a scrap of wood and secured with a clamp so that the bit doesn't splinter through the exit hole. The angle of the drill is checked by eye and/or with a try-square, and the drill is held and steadied with one hand and set in motion with the other.

dust-free Wood dust can irritate the skin and generally do damage to the eyes, ears, nose, and throat so try to keep the workshop environment dust-free. Sweep up daily, vacuum the worksurfaces after drilling and sawing, and be aware of the problem. Some woodworkers prefer to wear a mask while they are working.

Prior to painting or varnishing, make sure that the workpiece is completely free from wood dust. Sweep up the debris, vacuum the surfaces, and then wipe the workpiece over with a dampened cloth. Ideally, painting is best done in a special dust-free area that has been set aside for that purpose.

ear slots Having used a pencil and sticky tape to mark in the size and position of the slot, establish the width with a knife or saw cut, and then use a chisel to scoop out the curve-bottomed trench-like slot. Repeatedly slice down with the knife and scoop with the chisel until the slot is the correct depth.

files Files come in many shapes and sizes, everything from fine needle and riffler files through to large two-handed rasps. We tend to use open-toothed Surform rasps for large jobs, and sandpaper-wrapped-around-stick files for small details.

fillers Any soft putty-like dries-hard material used to fill tears, scratches, and cavities. We prefer to use a stable two-tube plastic/resin filler, one that can be sanded, sawn, and drilled. A good tip for small cavities is to make a filler with a mixture of scroll-saw dust and PVA adhesive.

finishing The process of filling, rubbing down, staining, painting, varnishing, waxing, and generally bringing the work to a satisfactory conclusion.

Forstner drill bit A drill bit used for boring out flat-bottomed holes in wood. Although Forstner bits are many times more expensive than regular spade/flat drill bits, they can be relied upon to produce accurate, perfect-every-time holes.

friction fit Components that can be pushed together for a smooth, tight fit. A tenon might be a good friction fit in a mortise, or a dowel might be a perfect fit in a wheel-hole. If the fit is such that the component needs to hammered into place, or is so loose that it falls out, then it cannot be described as a friction fit.

gents saw A small, round-handled, tenon-type, brass-backed saw, really good for making teddy bear toys. This saw usually has a blade about 10 inches long and about 20 fine-point teeth to the inch. Good for fine joints, cutting thin sections of plywood, and so on.

glues and adhesives We currently use PVA or *polyvinyl acetate* for large joints, dowel fixings, and mating flat surfaces, and Super Glue where we need to make a small, fast, very strong, dab-and-hold type joint.

gridded working drawing A drawing that has been drawn onto a scaled grid. If, for example, the scale of the grid is described as being "1 grid square to 1 inch," it simply means that each 1 of the grid squares can be read off and transferred as being a 1-inch unit of measurement. If you want to change the scale, all you do is draw up a larger grid, and transfer the image one square at a time.

hammer In the context of making relatively small teddy bear toys, we favor the use of a small, lightweight hammer called variously a pin, peen, or cross-peen hammer.

hardware Meaning all the nails, screws, washers, nuts, bolts, and hinges that you might need for a project. We use a lot of panel pins, brass screws, and nuts and bolts. For safety's sake, kids' playthings are best screwed, or at the very least glued and pin-fixed.

headstock In woodturning, the headstock is the power-driven unit at the lefthand side of the lathe. The central headstock spindle has an external screw-thread for chucks and faceplates, and an internal taper for the pronged center.

lathe A woodworking machine for cutting round sections. The wood is pivoted between centers, or held in a chuck, and spun against handheld cutting tool, such as a gouge or a chisel. The lathe is potentially an extremely dangerous piece of equipment, so you always need to be wide awake and ready for the unexpected.

Before you switch on the lathe always follow this checklist:

1. Make sure that the workpiece is well mounted and secure.
2. Turn the work over by hand and make sure that it is clear of the tool rest.
3. Tie back your hair, roll up your sleeves and generally make sure that you aren't going to get dragged into the lathe.
4. Make sure that children and pets are out of harm's way.
5. Make sure that all the tools are within reach but out of harm's way.
6. Make sure that the stop switch is operating and within easy reach.
7. Make sure that you can work without interruption.

When you have switched on the power always:

1. Stop the motor or at least slow down before testing with a template, dividers, or calipers.
2. Move the tool rest well out of the way before sanding.
3. Wear safety glasses and/or a dust mask.
4. Make sure that your chosen wood is nontoxic.
5. Hold all the tools firmly.
6. Never reach out over the lathe while it is running.

mating faces   The area between two touching parts, or two faces that are to be glued together.

masking tape   A sticky, low-tack adhesive, paper tape used for holding down working drawings, for strapping up work that has been glued, and so on.

modifying   The process of redesigning some part of the project to suit your own needs or likes. So for example, if you want to have the wheels bigger, then the design process of deciding whether or not the axle needs to be bigger, or the plywood thicker, or whatever, is described as "modifying."

movement   The sum total of all the moving parts—all the cams, washers, wheels, and rod that make up the project.

multicore plywood and multi-ply In the context of making toys, we always use best-quality, birch multicore or multi-veneer plywood. Such a plywood is commonly sold in thicknesses ranging from ⅛ inch through to 1 inch. It's more economical to purchase a whole 48-—96-inch sheet rather than small pieces. If you can only afford a single sheet, best to buy say the ¼-inch-thick ply, and then to sandwich/laminate layers to make ½ inch, ¾ inch, or whatever. Best-quality multicore plywood can easily be cut on a scroll saw, with all faces and edges being worked to a smooth and even finish.

Be warned: If you settle for using cheap-grade coarse-center plywood, it will be very difficult to work, and, as like as not, the laminations will break down and the cut edges will need filling.

offcuts Bits and pieces of scrap wood used for small jobs and for making prototypes. Offcuts might be left over from other projects or purchased from a wood supplier.

painting Ideally, the painting is best done in an area that has been set apart for that purpose. We use acrylics rather than model makers enamel/oil paints because they are user-friendly and nontoxic. Acrylics dry very quickly, several coats of paint can be applied in a short time, the brushes can be washed in water, and the colors are bright. The order of work is:

1. Start by making sure that the workpiece is smooth, clean, dry, and free from dust.
2. Spend time carefully setting out all your paints and materials.
3. Consider how the objects are going to be supported when they have been painted, and set up a line, or wire rack, or whatever.
4. Lay on a couple of base/ground coats.
5. Decorate with the fine-point details.
6. Finally, lay on a couple of coats of clear, high-shine varnish.

parting tool One of the primary woodturning tools—used for cutting trenches and parting the workpiece off from the lathe.

pencil-press transferring We use a soft 2B for designing and tracing, and a hard H for pencil-press transferring. The order of work is:

1. Draw out the full-size master design.
2. Take a careful tracing.
3. Pencil-over the lines at the back of the tracing with a 2B pencil.
4. Turn the tracing right-side-up and fix it to working surface of the wood with tabs of sticky tape.
5. Finally, rework the traced lines with a hard pencil.

pillar drill or drill press A large bench-mounted electric drill with a bit-gripping chuck and an adjustable height/angle worktable. If you reckon to make a lot of toys, then a drill of this character is a very useful piece of machinery.

pilot hole A small, drilled guide hole through which the blade of the scroll saw can be passed, or a hole used to ensure an easy passage for a screw.

pivot In the context of wooden teddy bear toys, a pivot is the point, rod, bolt, rivet, shaft or dowel, on which another part might swing, turn, roll or otherwise move.

plane A handheld tool used for smoothing and leveling wood. We use a small metal bench plane and a block plane.

pliers Pliers and grips come in many shapes and sizes. We use a pair of long-nosed pliers and a pair of locking grips.

profiles Any cutout, silhouette, cross section, drawn shape, flat-fretted form, or turning might be termed a profile.

prototype A working model made prior to making the actual toy. If you have doubts as to how such-and-such a toy is going to function, or if you have a mind to make a few changes, then you need to iron out possible problems by making a mock-up, working model, maquette, or prototype.

roughing out In woodturning, the initial swift stage of turning off the waste and achieving a round section. If you are using a small low-powered lathe, you will need to cut away some of the waste prior to mounting the wood on the lathe. The order of work is:

1. Establish the end centerpoints by drawing crossed diagonals.

2. Set the diameter of the turning by scribing the ends of the wood out with circles.
3. Draw tangents at the diagonal-circle crossover/intersection points.
4. Establish the waste by drawing lines from the resultant octagons and along the length of the wood.
5. Remove the bulk of the waste with a plane or draw knife.

rubbing down   The process of using sandpaper to rub the sawn profiles and sections down to a smooth, ready-to-paint finish. Working well away from the painting area, the order of work is:

1. Trim off the corners, edges, and burrs with a plane or chisel.
2. Swiftly rub over with a medium-grit sandpaper.
3. Fill cracks or holes with two-tube resin filler.
4. Finally, work through the pack of coarse-to-smooth graded sandpapers until the workpiece is smooth-to-the-touch. Be warned: If you are worried about breathing in potentially harmful dust, then wear a mask.

sanding   Sandpapers or glass papers are best purchased in graded packs, with the graded running in degrees of coarseness or *grits,* from rough-to-smooth. Small difficult-to-get-at areas are best worked with the sandpaper being supported on a stick tool.

screws and screwdrivers   In the context of making small teddy bear toys, screws are safer and more permanent than nails. If you have a choice, use brass screws with round heads, or brass screws with countersunk heads. Always make sure when you are finishing that the screws are smooth-to-the-touch and free from sharp edges and burrs. Use the correct-size screwdrivers so as to avoid doing damage to the workpiece and to the screw.

scroll saw   A fine-bladed, electric bench saw, sometimes called a *jig* or *fretsaw,* used for cutting out profiles in thin sheet wood, plastic, or metal. In use, the workpiece is pushed across the worktable and fed into the blade. The blades come in many grades and are cheap and easy to replace. The up-and-down jigging action of the blade results in a swift, fine, good-every-time cut.

Our scroll saw is a Hegner. It cuts anything from thin veneers through to 2-inch-thick wood, it is the perfect tool for teddy bear toymaking. The order of work for cutting out an enclosed hole or window is:

1. Release the blade tension and unhitch the top end of the blade.
2. Slide the workpiece on the cutting table and pass the blade through the pilot hole.
3. Refit the blade, adjust the tension and make sure that the worktable is set at the correct angle.
4. Switch on the power and feed the wood into the blade so that the line of cut is slightly to the waste side of the drawn line.
5. Remove the waste and unhitch the blade.

setting out   The act of transferring the working drawings through to the face of the wood and making initial cuts. See *pencils* and *pencil-press transferring*.

sharpening tools   All your cutting/edge tools need to be sharp. Ideally, you need a grindstone to reshape the bevel on a chipped or blunt edge, an oilstone for honing and rubbing down to a keen fine edge, and shaped slipstones to hone concave U-section gouges.

softwood   Meaning timber from a coniferous tree. It doesn't follow that softwoods are any softer or any easier to work than so-called hardwoods. We favor using three light-colored hardwoods: lime/linden and jelutong because they are so easy to carve and shape, and beech because it takes a crisp, hard-cornered finish.

steel ruler   A long, flexible tape measure, usually 6-10 feet long; very useful for measuring lengths of wood and around curved profiles.

stick-tools   Any "found" item used for supporting sandpaper might be termed a stick-tool. We tend to use such things as lolly sticks, broken hacksaw blades, and bits of dowel. In use, the sandpaper is held in place with pins or sticky tape, and then held and used like a file. See *sanding*.

straight saws   Any straight flat-bladed woodworking saw that does the job in hand.

templates A pattern or shape cut out from thin sheet wood or cardboard, that can be drawn around so as to reproduce a number of identical images. In the context of wood turning, for example, templates are used as a profile guide, with the waste wood being removed, until the template profile can be held for a close mating fit up against the wood being turned.

tracing paper A strong see-through paper used for transferring the lines of the design from the full-size master drawing through to the working face of the wood. When you come to trace off a design or pencil-press-transfer a design through to the wood, always make sure that the tracing paper is well secured with tabs of masking tape. See *pencils* and *press transferring*.

try square Also called a set square or simply a square, a tool used to test work for straightness and for 90° angles.

V-block A wooden block used to support round-section material. We usually make V-blocks from scrap wood to suit the job in hand. In use, the workpiece is cradled in the V, and held in place with a hold-down foot loop or with masking tape strapping.

varnish In the context of small wooden teddy bear toys (meaning toys that are painted and decorated with acrylic paints), it's best to use a clear, high-shine varnish.

vise A bench-mounted screw clamp, used for holding and securing the wood while it is being worked.

wheels There are ball-bead wheels, roller wheels, casters and glides. There are thin plastic wheels with spoked centers and black tires, fat wheels with rubber tires, fat wooden wheels, wheels made on the lathe, wheels fretted out on the scroll saw, and many sizes, types and forms in between. Some wheels are glue-fixed on the axles, others are fitted with screws and washers, and yet others are loose-fitted on stub axles. We usually sort out the size and type of the wheels right at the start of the project.

whittling From the Anglo Saxon word *thwitan,* meaning to cut and pare with a small knife. Many toymaking projects involve a small amount of whittling. Curves are cut back, dowel-ends are rounded, and so on. Currently we use a craft knife, a scalpel, and a penknife.

wood Timber and boards are the basic woodwork material. We favor using birch multicore plywood, beech, lime/linden and jelutong. When you are buying your wood, avoid material that looks to be stained, knotty, split, twisted or sappy. Spend time searching around for a piece that allows for the smallest possible amount of cutting waste. When we describe such-and-such a piece of wood as being "prepared," we mean a piece that has been planed on all edges and faces.

Although we usually specify wood that has been sized in multiples of ¼ inch and although we usually order wood to a preferred finished size, the norm is for wood to be planed to a nominal size. So for example, a piece of 3-—1-inch section wood might in actual fact measure 2⅞ × ⅞ inches.

woodturning tools Long-handled heavy-duty gouges and chisels used when turning wood on the lathe. We tend to use three primary tools: a round-nosed gouge, a skew chisel and a parting tool/chisel.

workbench A workbench might be just about anything from a worksurface out in the garage, through to the kitchen table, a side table in a spare room, or a purpose-built woodworking bench. Ideally, the toymaker's workbench needs to be strong, stable, at the correct height, clean, and fitted with a vise.

working drawings The scaled, measured, or full-size drawing, from which measurements are taken. See *designing*.

working face In the context of this book, the working face is the best side of the wood, the side that shows, the side that is going to be on view once the toy has been put together.

workout paper Paper on which all the pre-project notes, details, and sketches are worked out prior to actually getting to grips with the wood. We use a hardcover sketch book for all the initial designs and small details, and lengths of end-of-roll printers, paper/decorators, paper for the full-size patterns. Best save all your patterns for the next time around.

INDEX